PRE-HSE

MW00988107

Core Skills in Social Studies

New Readers Press
ProLiteracy's publishing division

Images:

Grateful acknowledgment is made for permission to reprint these original or copyrighted images:

p. 12 ©Bertl123; p. 24 ©Matt Gush; p. 29 ©Rob Crandall; p. 32 ©Dorling Kindersley; p. 35 ©Adrian Hancu; p. 39 ©American Progress by John Gast. Pictorial Press Ltd./Alamy; p. 40 ©JupiterImages; p. 41 ©casadaphoto; p. 42 ©Lefteris Papaulakis/Shutterstock; p. 48 ©photos.com; p. 50 ©North Wind Picture Archives/Alamy; p. 51 ©Howard Chandler Christy (1940)/GraphicaArtis/Corbis; p. 60 ©Library of Congress; p. 64 ©Everett Historical; p. 66 ©Everett Collection Inc./Alamy; p. 68 ©Heiko Kueverling; p. 70 ©NorGal/Shutterstock; p. 77 ©Digital Vision; p. 81 ©Mike Flippo; p. 85 ©Arogant; p. 89 ©Marco Rubino; p. 93 ©OSUCGA, The Ohio State University Billy Ireland Cartoon Library & Museum; p. 98 ©Ben Carlson; p. 104 ©John Moore; p. 110 ©Mary F. Calvert/ZUMAPRESS.com; p. 113 ©bikeriderlondon; p. 116 ©a katz/Shutterstock; p. 124 ©Rob Marmion; p. 125 ©Kzenon; p. 142 ©Library of Congress

Pre-HSE Core Skills in Social Studies
ISBN 978-1-56420-880-4

Developer: QuaraCORE
Editorial Director: Terrie Lipke
Cover Design: Carolyn Wallace
Technology Specialist: Maryellen Casey

CONTENTS

CONTENTS

Welcome to *Core Skills in Social Studies*, an important resource in helping you build a solid foundation of skills and content knowledge as you gear up to start preparing for the GED®, TASC, or HiSET® high school equivalency Social Studies test.

How to Use This Book

Pretest

The first step in using *Core Skills in Social Studies* is to take the Pretest, which begins on the next page. This test will show which skills you already have and which areas you need to practice. After taking the Pretest and checking your answers, use the chart on page 11 to find the lessons that will help you study the skills you need to improve.

Social Studies Skills Lessons

The book is organized into four units, each containing brief lessons that focus on the four areas of social studies: geography, history, civics, and economics. Read each of the lessons, which also include tips to help you understand skills and concepts:

- Connect to Today describes how concepts and historical events connect to our everyday lives.

- Skills Tips offer cues for easy ways to remember concepts and skills discussed in the lessons.

- Vocabulary Tips provide additional examples and other advice on using key terms.

Important vocabulary terms are listed under Key Terms on the first page of each lesson. These words appear in **boldface** when they are first used in each lesson. You can use the Glossary at the end of the book to look up definitions of key terms.

Each lesson ends with a brief Lesson Review with questions to test your knowledge of the content that was covered. Answers can be found in the Answer Key, beginning on page 150.

Each unit concludes with a Unit Practice Test that covers all the content in the unit's lessons. In the Answer Key, you will find explanations to help your understanding with many Unit Test questions.

Posttest

After completing all the units, you can test what you know by taking the Posttest, beginning on page 140. This test will help you check your understanding of all the skills in the book. It will also help determine if you are ready to move on to high school equivalency test preparation.

SOCIAL STUDIES PRETEST

Answer the following questions to test your knowledge of social studies content and skills.

1. A decrease in demand for high-definition televisions would lead to which change in the labor market in the television industry?

    A. An increase in supply of electronics makers would raise wages.

    B. A decrease in supply of television salespeople would lower wages.

    C. An increase in demand for cable television installers would raise wages.

    D. A decrease in demand for electronics workers would lower wages.

2. A supporter of limited government might oppose the Patient Protection and Affordable Care Act (Obamacare) for which of the following reasons?

    A. The Act gives too much power to individuals.

    B. The Act costs too much money.

    C. Citizens have too many choices of plans.

    D. The federal government does not have the power to be involved in health care.

3. Which of the following would BEST explain the usage of a referendum election?

    A. an attempt to remove a governor from office

    B. an attempt to propose a new law for the state legislature to review

    C. an attempt to overturn a tax law

    D. a chance to pick a new Congressperson

4. Which of the following emerged out of the Second Industrial Revolution?

    A. reform politics

    B. the assembly line

    C. settlement house movement

    D. recall vote

5. In order to keep prices as high as possible and safeguard its share of production, a trade cartel such as OPEC would implement which of the following policies?

    A. develop production agreements with non-OPEC nations

    B. limit the supply of oil throughout the world

    C. adopt a common currency for OPEC nations

    D. increase the supply of oil

6. When few houses are for sale in an area, real estate agents call this situation a "seller's market." Why is this term appropriate?

    A. Sellers can raise their prices when the supply of houses is high and demand is low.

    B. A person selling a house will accept an offer lower than the asking price when few homes are for sale but the demand is high.

    C. A lot of competition among sellers often raises the prices for houses.

    D. Sellers usually have an advantage in this kind of real estate market.

7. If a geographer wanted to show a three-dimensional representation of the earth and its features, the best tool to use would be which of the following?

    A. map

    B. satellite photograph

    C. GPS system

    D. globe

8. A person in favor of suffrage for women and young adult Americans would support which constitutional amendments?

    A. Nineteenth and Twenty-third

    B. Fourteenth and Twenty-sixth

    C. Nineteenth and Twenty-sixth

    D. Fourteenth and Nineteenth

9. Which statement best summarizes the similarities between the Supreme Court cases *Plessy* v. *Ferguson* and *Brown* v. *Board of Education*?

   A. Both cases involved the rights of students in public education.

   B. Both cases denied African Americans' rights.

   C. Both cases affirmed the rights of women.

   D. Both cases involved the policy of segregation.

10. Which of the following phrases best describes the concept behind collective bargaining strategies used by labor unions?

   A. to each his or her own

   B. strength in numbers

   C. divide and conquer

   D. power of the corporation

11. President Thomas Jefferson acquired a huge amount of land that almost doubled the size of the United States. What was this land acquisition called?

   A. The Louisiana Purchase

   B. The Missouri Compromise

   C. The California Gold Rush

   D. The Treaty of Guadalupe-Hidalgo

12. Which summary best describes American federalism?

   A. The national government has absolute powers.

   B. The federal government is allowed to change the Constitution as it sees fit.

   C. States maintain complete control over the actions of the federal government.

   D. National and state governments share powers.

13. What is the name of the important trade routes that connected Asia to the Mediterranean region in the 1200s?

   A. Muslim Corridor

   C. China Highways

   B. Silk Roads

   D. Dynastic Paths

14. Which statement best explains the difference between a natural-born citizen and a naturalized citizen?

   A. A naturalized citizen acquires citizenship after living in the United States for three years; a natural-born citizen is born to parents who moved to the United States.

   B. A natural-born citizen is born in one of the 50 states; a naturalized citizen is born in a U.S. territory.

   C. A naturalized citizen acquires citizenship after serving in the military; natural-born citizens acquire citizenship if an ancestor served in the armed forces.

   D. A natural-born citizen acquires citizenship at birth; a naturalized citizen is born a citizen of another country before acquiring U.S. citizenship.

15. Which of the following is an example of an opportunity cost?

   A. the amount of vacation time lost while you played in a softball tournament instead

   B. the money spent on the purchase a new car

   C. the additional cost of purchasing something valuable

   D. the amount of money a producer needs to manufacture a new product

Complete each sentence with the appropriate term.

16. The first 10 amendments to the U.S. Constitution are known as _____

SOCIAL STUDIES PRETEST

17. The imaginary line that divides Earth into the northern and southern hemispheres is called the

    _____

18. Democracy was first developed in ancient

    _____

19. The average weather in a place over time is called

    _____

20. African Americans, Native Americans, women, and Hispanic Americans all protested and worked to secure their _____ in the 1950s through the 1970s.

21. A politician who helps write laws would be a member of the _____ branch of government.

Complete each sentence with one of the terms listed. Use each term one time.

Middle Colonies	Columbian Exchange
Mayflower Compact	Southern Colonies

22. The Pilgrims signed a document called the _____, the first framework of government in America.

23. The movement of plants, animals, and diseases between Europe and the Americas during the fifteenth and sixteenth centuries is called the

    _____

24. Boston and New York were important cities in the

    _____

25. Slave labor in the _____ was a key driver of the economy.

26. Sort the following events into the correct chronological order.

A. Reconstruction	**C.** Emancipation Proclamation
B. States secede	**D.** President Lincoln assassinated

    [1] → [2] → [3] → [4]

Use the following information to answer questions 27–28.

Geographers count the number of people who live in a place. They also gather various data about those people. For example, geographers count the number of babies born in a certain year. The number of babies born per 1,000 people gives that population's birth rate. The death rate is the number of people who die per 1,000 people in a year. Comparing the birth rate and the death rate shows how much a population is growing naturally.

27. What general conclusion can you make about a population that has a higher birth rate than death rate?

    _____

28. What general conclusion can you make about a population that has a low birth rate and a higher death rate?

    _____

Read the following passage, and then answer the question that follows.

By July 1788, all the states except Rhode Island and North Carolina had ratified the Constitution. Consequently, the new government was launched, and Congress planned its first meeting.

29. Based on the information in the passage, the meaning of the word *ratified* is

    _____

    _____

30. Add each of the following events to the timeline to show the correct sequence of events.

    A. European empires are formed in the Americas

    B. Greeks form city-states

    C. Renaissance emerges in Europe

    D. Irrigation systems are developed

    E. Scientific Revolution sweeps Europe

    ┬──────┬──────┬──────┬──────┬──────

Identify where each Native American group lived by filling in each blank with North America, South America, *or* Central America.

31. Mississippian _____

32. Aztec _____

33. Iroquois _____

34. Maya _____

35. Inca _____

Use the following graph to answer questions 36–37.

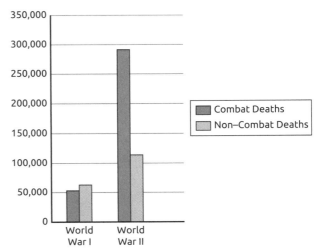

U.S. Battle Deaths: World War I and World War II

Source: Dept. of Veteran Affairs

36. Which of the following is a conclusion that can be drawn from the graph about World War I?

    A. Combat was not the leading cause of death for Americans in World War I.

    B. More Americans died in combat than in non-combat.

    C. Combat deaths were half of non-combat deaths.

    D. Combat and non-combat deaths were roughly the same.

37. Which of the following is a conclusion that can be drawn from the graph about World War II?

    A. Combat was not the leading cause of death for Americans in World War II.

    B. Combat death numbers in World War II were similar to those of World War I.

    C. Combat deaths were more than twice the number of non-combat deaths.

    D. Americans suffered fewer casualties in World War II than in World War I.

1. D.
2. D.
3. C.
4. B.
5. B.
6. D.
7. D.
8. C.
9. D.
10. B.
11. A.
12. D.
13. B.
14. D.
15. A.
16. the Bill of Rights
17. equator
18. Greece
19. climate
20. civil rights
21. legislative
22. Mayflower Compact
23. Columbian Exchange
24. Middle Colonies
25. Southern Colonies
26.

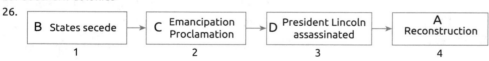

27. Sample answer: The population will most likely grow.
28. Sample answer: The population will probably decrease.
29. approved, or agreed to
30.

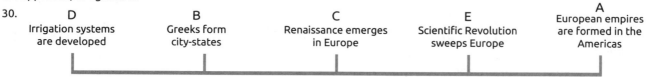

31. North America
32. Central America
33. North America
34. Central America
35. South America
36. A.
37. C.

Check your answers. Review the questions you did not answer correctly. You can use the following chart to locate lessons in this book that will help you learn more about those social studies content and skills. Which lessons do you need to study? Work through the book, paying close attention to the lessons in which you missed the most questions. At the end of the book, you will have a chance to take another test to see how much your score improves.

Question	Where to Look for Help		
	Unit	Lesson	Page
1, 6	4	2, 3, 4	127
2	3	12	115
3	3	10	109
4	2	7	60
5	4	5	135
7	1	1	12
8	3	9	106
9	3	11	112
10	4	4	133
11, 25	2	5	54
12	3	5	94
13	1	8	34
14	3	8	103
15	4	1	124
16, 29	3	2	81
17	1	2	16
18, 30	1	7	31
19	1	5	26
20	2	9	66
21	3	4	89
22, 24	2	2	43
23, 31, 32, 33, 34, 35	2	1	39
26	2	6	57
27, 28	1	3	20
36, 37	2	8	63

UNIT 1

Geography and the World

One morning you read a news story online. It tells about a political event happening in a distant place. You may never have been to this place. If you know about geography, however, you can have some ideas about what life is like there. Geography can tell you about the place's land, people, and culture. It even helps you think about what kinds of work people there do and what everyday problems they may have.

Geography is more than just maps. Understanding the relationship between people and places will help you better understand the world around you. It will also help you understand history and economics.

Study the photo of Istanbul, Turkey. It shows physical geographic features like water and hills. It also shows human geographic features suggesting the cultural characteristics of its people.

GEOGRAPHY AND GEOGRAPHIC TOOLS

What Is Geography?

Geographers do all kinds of jobs. They may interpret weather predictions or study floods and earthquakes, for example. They may also analyze political information or help plan the growth of cities. No matter their work, all geographers rely on certain tools.

Geography is the study of Earth and its people. Geographers divide geography into smaller areas of study. **Physical geography** investigates physical features and processes. **Human geography** analyzes how people interact with places. A human geographer may investigate the ways that people have changed the land by building farms and cities.

Human geography can also be divided into smaller areas of study. Cultural geography, for example, considers characteristics such as religion or language. The study of government and elections is part of political geography. Economic geography looks into how and where people work and conduct trade. Sometimes, these different kinds of geographic study overlap.

Using Geographic Tools

Geographers use many tools to view and analyze Earth. One common tool is a **map**. Maps show Earth's features using a flat surface. Because Earth is a sphere, maps cannot show it exactly as it is. Map makers use different **map projections** to address this problem. Map projections all have some distortion, or error, in their representations. **Globes** are three-dimensional spheres that show Earth and its features. Globes represent Earth more accurately than maps do.

Mercator and Gall-Peters Projections

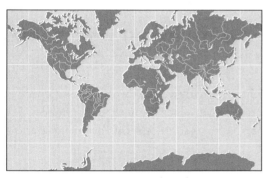

Mercator Projection

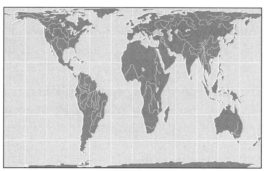

Gall-Peters Projection

These maps show the Mercator Projection (left) and Gall-Peters Projection (right). What differences do you see in how these projections show Earth?

Key Terms

compass rose

geography

global positioning system (GPS)

globe

human geography

map

map projection

physical geography

scale

Vocabulary Tip

Use word parts to help find the meanings of unfamiliar words. The word *geography* has two main word parts. *Geo-* means Earth. Whenever you see a word that begins with *geo-*, it probably has a meaning about Earth. The word part *graph* means *write*, so it often appears in words about writing or studying.

GEOGRAPHY AND GEOGRAPHIC TOOLS

Skills Tip

Geographers create different kinds of maps depending on what information they want to show. Physical maps show features like continents, rivers, and mountains. Political maps show borders and cities. Resource maps show important natural resources like minerals or crops. Historical maps show information about events in the past. Population maps show how many people live in certain places. What other kinds of maps can you think of?

Map keys give important information about the maps they accompany. Keys tell the symbols used on a map and their meanings. Many maps, for example, use dots to show cities and black lines to show borders. Special kinds of maps use symbols specific to their purposes. A park map may use a tent to show a campground and picnic tables to show park shelters. A road map may have a symbol of a road cone to show construction areas.

Along with keys, maps usually have two features to help users interpret their physical geography. A map **scale** shows how distance is represented on a map. A map of the world probably has a large scale with many miles or kilometers per inch. A map of a community college campus has a small scale to help users find specific buildings or rooms. Most maps also have a **compass rose**. This tells how the map is oriented by indicating directions such as north and south. Maps are often—but not always—oriented so that north is at the top.

Map Key Example

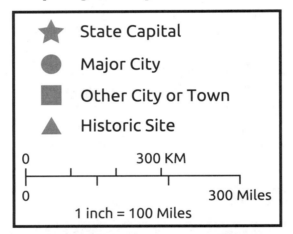

Study the map key to figure out each symbol's meaning. What does a star show on this map?

The **global positioning system (GPS)** uses satellites high above Earth to pinpoint exact locations. People today rely on GPS to get directions from place to place. Cell phone applications and car navigation systems use GPS. GPS is also important for business and military uses.

Complete the activities below to check your understanding of the lesson content. The Unit 1 Answer Key is on page 150.

Vocabulary

Match each key word with its definition.

1. physical geography
2. global positioning system (GPS)
3. human geography
4. scale
5. geography
6. map projection

A. study of how people relate to Earth

B. study of Earth and its people

C. way of showing Earth on a flat surface

D. study of features like mountains and rivers

E. map tool showing distance

F. technology using satellites to find exact locations

Skills Practice

Study the map. Then write complete sentences to answer the questions that follow.

7. What kind of map is this, and how can you tell?

   _____

8. According to this map, what are two large cities in Missouri?

   _____

9. What map-reading tool is missing from this map that should be added? How would that tool help users interpret the map?

   _____

10. Suppose you wanted to use this map in a presentation about the history of Missouri. What is one additional type of information you could add to this map to help your presentation?

    _____

GLOBAL AND U.S. REGIONS

Key Terms

continent

Equator

formal region

functional region

hemisphere

latitude

longitude

perceptual region

Prime Meridian

region

Vocabulary Tip

Remember that a region can include any area with a shared characteristic. This means that the boundaries of a region may not match state or national borders. Apply the term *region* flexibly as you study geography.

What Is a Region?

How do geographers organize the diverse places on Earth? Often, they use regions. Understanding regions will help you think like a geographer. It will also help you understand other social studies topics.

Regions are a way to organize places on Earth. A region includes areas with a certain shared characteristic. Regions can reflect physical geography. For example, geographers may study climate regions with similar weather patterns. Or they may study landform regions, such as mountain ranges. Regions can also reflect human geography. Ethnic regions and language regions are both examples of this.

Geographers often organize regions into three categories. **Formal regions** have specific boundaries set either by nature or by people. An ocean lies within a formal region set by its physical extent. The borders of a state create a formal region established by the government. A **functional region** includes all the areas near a place that work together. A city and its suburbs are one common kind of functional region. A **perceptual region** is a region that exists because people think about all the places within it as being similar. Perceptual regions are also known as vernacular regions. The borders of these regions may vary based on an individual's ideas about places. The South, for example, is a perceptual region.

Regions can change over time. A city that adds nearby land changes the boundaries of its formal region. The movement of Spanish-speaking people from Mexico and Central America to the United States is changing the boundaries of language regions. Melting glaciers may raise sea levels and change the boundaries of oceans. Places can belong to more than one region. Regions can also overlap.

U.S. Regions

The United States is a huge country. Geographers and historians often divide the United States into regions. This helps them analyze smaller areas. It also helps show how physical and human geography makes places different. Often, people organize the United States into four regions. These include the Northeast, the Southeast, the Midwest, and the West. Smaller regions lie within each main region. For example, the region of New England is part of the Northeast. The Southwest is part of the West.

Some regions cross the four main regions. For example, the Rust Belt is an economic region. It includes places in the Midwest and Northeast that once had strong manufacturing industries but have struggled to succeed as manufacturing has declined. The Sun Belt is a climate region. It includes places across the Southeast and West that have many sunny days and pleasant temperatures.

U.S. Regions

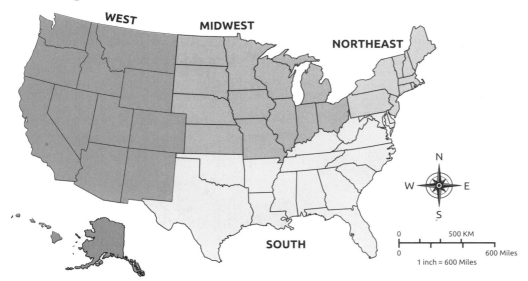

Geographers at the U.S. Census divide the country into four regions. Are these formal, functional, or perceptual regions?

Skills Tip

Learning to identify regions and patterns in maps will help you analyze them. First, study the map and its key to see if any shading or color is used to show information. Then, look for labels that tell about different parts of the map. Finally, consider how the parts you found relate to one another. Look for borders or overlapping sections. Determine whether one region is larger than another.

Global Regions

Geographers often look at regions within and across Earth's **continents**. Continents are large landmasses. Earth has seven continents. These are North America, South America, Europe, Asia, Africa, Australia, and Antarctica. Some geographers combine Europe and Asia into one continent called Eurasia. This is because they are actually part of one landmass.

Earth has other geographic regions that do not exactly match with the continents. These regions share human characteristics like language, religion, or history. Central America lies along a narrow strip of land connecting North and South America. The Caribbean includes the small islands lying to the east of Central America. The small islands of the Pacific Ocean are called Oceania. A large region of Southwest Asia is known as the Middle East. Sometimes, parts of North Africa, north of the Sahara Desert, are included in this region. The rest of Africa is known as Sub-Saharan Africa.

Another way that geographers organize Earth into regions is by using **latitude** and **longitude**. These are sets of imaginary lines that encircle Earth. Latitude lines lie horizontally, and longitude lines lie vertically. Both sets are measured in degrees from special central lines. The **Equator** is the central line of latitude. Geographers measure outward north and south from the Equator. The **Prime Meridian** is the central line of longitude. Geographers measure outward east and west from the Prime Meridian.

GLOBAL AND U.S. REGIONS

The Equator and Prime Meridian separate Earth into **hemispheres**. A hemisphere is one-half of Earth. The Equator divides Earth into the Northern and Southern Hemispheres. North America and Europe lie entirely in the Northern Hemisphere. Australia and Antarctica lie entirely in the Southern Hemisphere. Africa, Asia, and South America lie in both. The Prime Meridian divides Earth into the Western and Eastern Hemispheres.

World Map

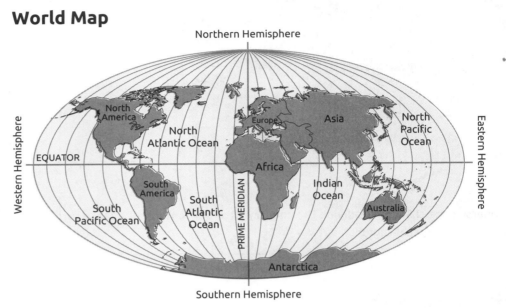

The Equator and Prime Meridian divide Earth into hemispheres. Which continents are in the Western Hemisphere? Which continents are in the Eastern Hemisphere?

LESSON REVIEW

Complete the activities below to check your understanding of the lesson content. The Unit 1 Answer Key is on page 150.

Vocabulary

Write definitions in your own words for each of the key terms.

1. continent _____

   _____

2. hemisphere _____

   _____

3. latitude _____

   _____

4.   Prime Meridian _____

_____

5.   region _____

_____

Apply Your Knowledge

Label each region as a formal, functional, or perceptual region.

6.   Midwest _____

7.   State of California _____

8.   Rust Belt _____

9.   New York City metropolitan area _____

10. Eastern Hemisphere _____

11. Middle East _____

Skills Practice

Use the map to complete the activity. Answer the question using complete sentences.

The World

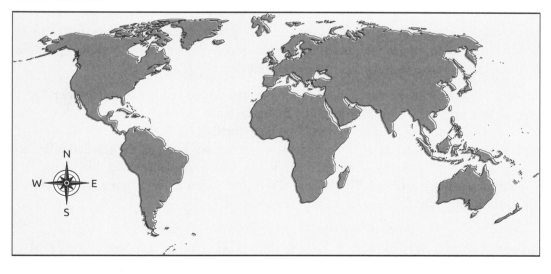

12. Label the following continents: North America, South America, Africa, and Asia.

13. Add the four hemispheres to the map.

14. Add the Prime Meridian and Equator to the map. What is the purpose of these features?

_____

_____

Key Terms

birth rate

crime rate

death rate

demographics

immigration

literacy rate

population

population pyramid

Skills Tip

Demographic information is often presented numerically in a chart, graph, or table. Begin studying a graphic by reading the title. Note the main purpose of the graphic. See whether it covers a certain time period. Then, carefully review each row, column, or axis heading. These will tell you exactly what information each piece of data gives.

Populations and Demographics

A **population** includes all the people who live in a place. Geographers study populations in order to learn more about what life is like in different places.

Demographics is the study and analysis of population data. Geographers analyze many different kinds of data to learn about populations. They count the number of people who live in a place. They also gather lots of data about those people. For example, geographers count the number of babies born in a certain year. The number of babies born per 1,000 people gives that population's **birth rate**. Geographers also count the number of people who die. The **death rate** is the number of people who die per 1,000 people in a year.

Putting these pieces of data together allows geographers to draw important conclusions. Comparing the birth rate and the death rate shows how much a population is growing naturally. A population with a higher birth rate than death rate will almost certainly grow over time. But a population with a low birth rate and higher death rate may decrease.

Immigration can boost a decreasing population. Immigration is the movement of people from one place to another in order to live there. To find the immigration rate, geographers can measure how many people come to settle in a place

Demographic data can also tell what life is like. Geographers measure how well educated people are by finding the **literacy rate**. This counts the number of people over the age of 15 who can read and write. Studying the number of crimes shows the **crime rate**. This tells how safe a place is to live and work. Geographers may even measure how large people's homes are or whether they own bicycles or cars.

Showing Populations Graphically

Demographic data may be shown in a chart or graph. One special tool for showing populations is a **population pyramid**. A population pyramid shows the overall population. It divides them into groups by age range and gender.

A population with a large base and small top has many young people and few older people. This suggests a high birth rate and high death rate. This type of pyramid is common in developing nations such as Nigeria. Industrialized nations often have low birth rates and low death rates. They have pyramids that are wider at the top and relatively smaller at the bottom. Japan is one example of this. Many people live long lives in the United States. But the nation also has a medium birth rate and receives many immigrants. This makes its pyramid somewhat equal.

Geographers can use population pyramids to analyze overall populations and trends. A population pyramid like Nigeria's suggests that people have poor nutrition and health care. This keeps them from living long lives. A pyramid like Japan's gives evidence that people have small families. A nation that had lost many young men fighting in a war may show a much shorter bar for men of a certain age.

Population Graphs

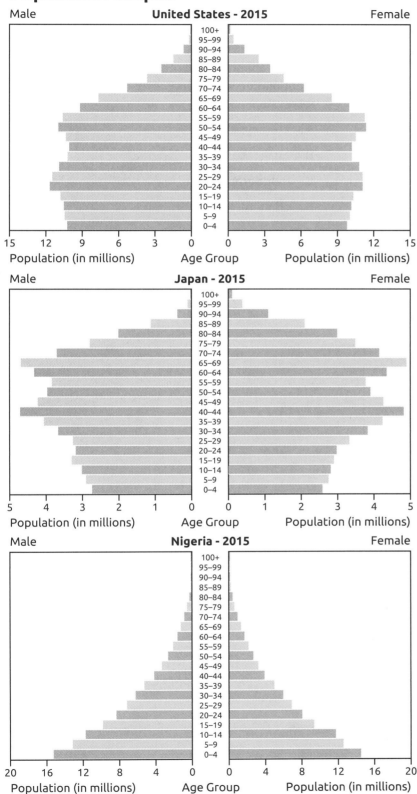

Population pyramids for the United States, Japan, and Nigeria.

Complete the activities below to check your understanding of the lesson content. The Unit 1 Answer Key is on page 150.

Vocabulary

Choose the correct answer to each question.

1. What is the best definition of demographics?

   A. tool showing population by age and gender

   B. number of people who live in a place

   C. study of population data

   D. difference between birth and death rate

2. A geographer who wanted to determine whether a population would grow over time would be most interested in its

   A. literacy rate.

   B. birth rate.

   C. demographic rate.

   D. crime rate.

Skills Practice

Study the population pyramid. Then write complete sentences to answer the questions that follow.

Population Pyramid of Indonesia

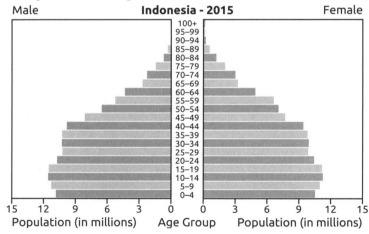

3. What age groups in Indonesia have the highest population?

   _____

   _____

4. Based on this population pyramid, what prediction can you make about Indonesia's population growth over time? Explain your answer.

   _____

   _____

5. Based on this population pyramid, what conclusion can you draw about health care in Indonesia?

   _____

   _____

Types of Natural Resources

Look at the items around you. Where did they come from? Practically everything people use in everyday life—even plastic—got its start as a natural resource.

Natural resources include any useful material provided by Earth. Crops grown for food are natural resources. So are water, air, forests, and minerals. People can harness natural resources to power homes or grow food. They can also extract natural resources from Earth through mining or drilling. Natural resources provide **raw materials** that can be turned into other products.

Humans have relied on natural resources for thousands of years. Everyone needs clean water supplies for drinking, cooking, and bathing. Fertile soil allows humans to grow crops and raise animals for food. People use wood to build homes and make fires. Crops such as cotton are turned into cloth. Places with access to ample natural resources are easier for people to live in.

Beginning in the 1700s, people especially looked to natural resources for manufacturing and industry. The first factories relied on rushing rivers to generate water power. They also used coal, a mineral made of hardened carbon, for fuel. Burning coal provides a lot of power. In time, people also began burning oil for power. Oil comes from a liquid substance that takes millions of years to form under Earth's surface. Resources like coal and oil are known as **fossil fuels**. Fossil fuels come from carbon deposits left by decaying life forms from long ago. Because they take so long to form, they are **non-renewable resources**.

People today are looking to new ways to generate energy. Solar power collects energy from the sun using special panels to soak up heat and light. Wind power is an old idea. The movement of air turns windmills, harnessing their force for human use. Both solar power and wind power are **renewable resources**.

Problems of Resource Use

Resources provide humans with valuable benefits. Resource use can create problems, too. One main problem of resource use is **pollution**. Pollution is any harmful substance that occurs in the environment.

Using resources can create air pollution or water pollution. Air pollution happens when factories or power plants burn some types of fuel. It also happens when cars emit exhaust fumes from burning gasoline in their engines. Other human activities can cause air pollution, too. Chemicals and cleaning supplies can also contribute to air pollution. Most air pollution makes the air people breathe thick and dirty. Visible air pollution is called **smog**.

Water pollution is another serious problem of resource use. Polluted water may harm plant and animal life. It is also unsafe for humans to drink. Air pollution and water pollution can be closely related. Polluted air is gathered in the clouds. When it rains, the clouds pass this pollution back down to Earth through rain droplets. Factories, landfills, and other human activities can also pollute water.

Key Terms

Environmental Protection Agency

fossil fuel

natural resource

non-renewable resource

pollution

raw materials

recycle

renewable resource

smog

Skills Tip

To describe a process, first read the text to find details about your topic. Then, look for ways that people, places, events, or ideas interact. Finding these connections will help you figure out how and why processes or events took place. Then, restate the process in your own words. Be sure to include the most important details or relationships in your description.

Connect to Today

Does your household have a recycling bin? People all around the United States look closely at their trash to sort out items that could be recycled. Recyclable goods may have special markings on them. Plastic containers, for example, have numbers to show what they are made of. This determines whether they can be recycled. Your recycled soda bottle may become new carpeting or even a fleece sweatshirt!

This symbol marks an item that can be recycled. How else can you tell if something is recyclable?

Governments, organizations, and individuals are all working to control pollution. People can **recycle**. Recycling is sending garbage to be reused as a new item. The U.S. government created the **Environmental Protection Agency (EPA)** in the 1970s. This agency monitors air and water pollution. People are also turning to renewable energy resources like wind or solar power. These do not create pollution.

Smog is one type of air pollution. It affects many large U.S. cities, such as Los Angeles.

Complete the activities below to check your understanding of the lesson content. The Unit 1 Answer Key is on page 150.

Vocabulary

Write definitions in your own words for each of the key terms.

1. fossil fuel _____

_____

2. pollution _____

_____

3. renewable resource _____

_____

4. smog _____

_____

Apply Your Knowledge

Choose the correct answer to each question.

5. One example of a fossil fuel is

   A. plastics.

   B. wind power.

   C. solar power.

   D. petroleum.

6. According to the lesson, which of these is a benefit of recycling?

   A. less pollution and waste

   B. increased fossil fuel use

   C. more technological discovery

   D. lower costs for resources

Skills Practice

Write a sentence or two to describe each process listed below.

7. air pollution

_____

_____

_____

8. water pollution

_____

_____

_____

Key Terms

average

climate

climate change

deforestation

glacier

greenhouse gas

hurricane

precipitation

tornado

weather

Weather and Climate

Everyone cares about the weather. Many people check forecasts every day. Weather and climate are both common ways that geography affects people's lives.

Weather is the atmospheric conditions in a place at any given time. Weather includes temperature, humidity, wind, and whether it is dry or raining. **Climate** shows a place's average weather over time. A desert, for example, has a hot and dry climate. Geographers identify several different types of climate zones across Earth. These are based mostly on temperature and precipitation. **Precipitation** includes rain and snowfall.

U.S. Climate Zones

COOL

TEMPERATE

HOT-HUMID

HOT-ARID

The United States covers several climate zones. Based on this map, what conclusion can you draw about the differences in climate between Texas and Pennsylvania?

Sometimes, weather can result in damage to humans and their environments. **Hurricanes** are strong storms that form in the Atlantic Ocean. Hurricanes have heavy rains and strong winds. In 2005, Hurricane Katrina caused flooding and great damage to the city of New Orleans. **Tornados** also form from storms. They are huge columns of spinning air that can go as fast as 300 miles per hour. If they touch down in populated places, tornados can destroy buildings and injure or kill people. Most tornados in the United States are much weaker, though.

Humans try to prepare for strong weather events, in part, by changing their environments. People have built levees, a kind of sea wall, along coasts where flooding may happen. They build strong houses with thick walls and durable roofs in tornado country.

Climate Change

Earth is a constantly changing place. Its crust moves and causes earthquakes. Rain or drought may cause river or ocean levels to rise and fall. Changes in Earth's atmosphere can cause **climate change**. Climate change is a long-term shift in temperatures and other weather conditions.

Scientists today worry that humans are causing Earth's climate to change in a way that will hurt people. Burning fossil fuels like coal and oil releases **greenhouse gases**. All greenhouse gases trap heat in Earth's atmosphere. The main greenhouse gas released in the United States is carbon dioxide. Trees and other plants change carbon dioxide into oxygen. But **deforestation**, or the widespread cutting down of trees, is spreading as Earth's population grows. This means fewer plants exist to absorb harmful gases.

Over time, changes in the atmosphere cause Earth's overall temperature to warm. The change in temperature may be only a few degrees Fahrenheit. But small changes can have a big impact. Scientists point to the decreasing size of **glaciers** near Antarctica as one main effect. Glaciers are large, thick sheets of ice. As glaciers melt, the water that was frozen within them is released into the ocean. This raises sea levels, which could cause flooding and make low-lying cities hard to live in.

People have strong opinions about climate change. The methods needed to slow or stop the release of greenhouse gases are expensive. They also require people to change the way they live. Governments, companies, and individuals are often reluctant to tackle the challenge because of these issues.

Source: Washington State Department of Ecology

Greenhouse gases trap heat from the Sun in Earth's atmosphere. How does an increase in gases trap more heat?

Complete the activities below to check your understanding of the lesson content. The Unit 1 Answer Key is on page 150.

Vocabulary

Match each key word with its definition.

1. climate
2. greenhouse gas
3. precipitation
4. deforestation
5. climate change
6. glacier

A. substance that traps heat in Earth's atmosphere
B. large, thick sheet of ice
C. long-term shift in weather over time
D. average weather in a place over time
E. cutting down of trees and plants
F. rain or snowfall

Skills Practice

Study the data set. Then complete the sentences with the correct answer.

Average High and Low Temperatures in F°, Atlanta, GA												
	Jan	**Feb**	**Mar**	**Apr**	**May**	**Jun**	**Jul**	**Aug**	**Sept**	**Oct**	**Nov**	**Dec**
High	52	57	65	73	80	86	89	88	82	73	64	54
Low	34	38	44	52	60	68	71	71	65	54	45	37

7. The average high temperature in Atlanta for the months of June, July, and August is _____ degrees F.

8. The median low temperature in Atlanta for the months of January, February, and March is _____ degrees F.

9. The mode of low temperatures in Atlanta for the entire year is _____ degrees F.

GLOBALIZATION

Causes of Globalization

Have you ever heard someone say that the world is getting smaller? This is not physically true. But people are more connected now than ever before.

Globalization is the interconnectedness of people, technology, and ideas around the world. People have experienced globalization for centuries. Trade and exploration carried goods and ideas worldwide as early as the 1500s. However, the pace of globalization sped up greatly during the late 1900s.

Transportation and communication are the keys to globalization. Airplanes, telephones, and the Internet allow **multinational corporations** to operate all around the world. Television and movies spread culture far from its source.

The Internet allows for nearly instant communication across long distances. The United States first developed the Internet for military use. During the 1990s, however, it became more common for people to use the Internet at home, work, or school. Some places do not have the **infrastructure** for computers to access the Internet. Infrastructure is the systems connecting people, like power lines and roads. But people in these places may access the Internet through mobile networks.

Key Terms

globalization

infrastructure

McDonaldization

multinational corporation

One effect of globalization is the spread of U.S. tastes around the world.

Effects of Globalization

Globalization has made the world's people and economies more connected. You probably have clothing and shoes made by workers from all over the world. You may play video games coded by people in Russia or Singapore. These are results of economic globalization. Globalization has also encouraged more and more people to learn to speak English. People in Africa and Japan enjoy American music and eat cheeseburgers. The spread of U.S. culture and tastes around the world is known as **McDonaldization**.

Some people worry that globalization causes problems. People around the world enjoy American food, entertainment, and products. But this may discourage them from keeping their own culture alive. Large corporations bring jobs all over the world. But they may not understand local practices. They may also pay workers poorly or make them work in harsh conditions.

Skills Tip

Many social studies texts give more than one set of ideas about a certain event or process. When reading these texts, look closely for sets of different ideas. Ask yourself why different groups may think the way they do. According to this text, why do people disagree about globalization? What does this suggest about their experiences and beliefs?

Complete the activities below to check your understanding of the lesson content. The Unit 1 Answer Key is on page 150.

Vocabulary

Write definitions in your own words for each of the key terms.

1. globalization _____

_____

2. infrastructure _____

_____

3. McDonaldization _____

_____

4. multinational corporation _____

_____

Skills Practice

Read the text below. Then respond to the prompt.

> Globalization, as defined by rich people like us, is a very nice thing . . . . you are talking about the Internet, you are talking about cell phones, you are talking about computers. This doesn't affect two-thirds of the people of the world.
>
> —Former U.S. President Jimmy Carter

5. Write a paragraph in which you develop an argument supporting or opposing the speaker's central idea. Incorporate specific evidence from the lesson and your own knowledge to support your analysis.

_____

_____

_____

_____

_____

_____

_____

_____

_____

_____

_____

_____

Long ago, people lived by hunting and gathering. The development of agriculture allowed humans to form societies. Over thousands of years, those early civilizations transformed. They became our world today.

First Human Civilizations

Climate changes made farming possible about 15,000 years ago. Historians believe people had established permanent farming settlements by about 9000 BCE. The first were near what are now Iraq and Syria. This area is known as Mesopotamia. Other people around the world also later developed farming. People found ways to make farming easier over time. For example, they used **irrigation** systems to water crops.

Farming created extra food to feed people who were not farmers themselves. This allowed some people to take other jobs. They become government officials or merchants, for example. Cities and empires grew up as a result. Sumer, Babylonia, and Egypt were important early civilizations. People there wrote laws, conducted trade, and built large temples and pyramids.

Early societies advanced human knowledge. They developed early forms of writing using symbols or letters. They began to study medicine and science. These ideas spread over time as people moved and traded over long distances.

Greece and Rome

By about 500 BCE, the area near the Mediterranean Sea became a center of civilization. The ancient Greeks formed several independent **city-states**. These places had some shared cultural characteristics. But each city-state had its own government. Athens and Sparta are the two most famous city-states. Athens is the home of **democracy**. Its government allowed all citizens to vote on decisions or be elected to office. Sparta had a strong military.

Alexander the Great came from an area near Greece called Macedonia. His father conquered the Greek city-states in the 300s BCE. Alexander then led armies as far east as India. He brought Greek ideas and knowledge throughout the region.

The Romans came to rule much of the Mediterranean, the Middle East, and Western Europe. Rome established a huge empire that lasted for hundreds of years. Romans encouraged trade, built roads, and kept places peaceful. Maintaining such a large empire was hard, however. Internal problems and invasions weakened the empire. It collapsed in 476 CE.

Development of Europe

Life changed in Europe after the fall of Rome. Countries there were no longer part of an empire. Kings did not always have strong power over their lands. Most people worked as peasant farmers for local lords. In 1215, the English king signed the **Magna Carta**. This document limited the monarch's powers and protected some rights of citizens.

During the 1400s, parts of Europe experienced a new interest in culture and knowledge. This was called the **Renaissance**. The Renaissance was especially strong in Italy.

Key Terms

- city-state
- democracy
- Enlightenment
- imperialism
- irrigation
- Magna Carta
- Reformation
- Renaissance
- Scientific Revolution

Skills Tip

Finding an author's central idea will help you better understand a text. Many texts state their central ideas directly at the beginning or end. Notice that this section of text begins with the statement *By about 500 BCE, the area near the Mediterranean Sea became a center of civilization.* All the other details in this section tell about this central idea. If the central idea is not stated directly, you can still figure it out. Look for the most important ideas in the text. Then decide what central idea they all support.

TURNING POINTS IN WORLD HISTORY—THE WEST

Artists looked to ancient Greece and Rome for inspiration. The invention of the printing press helped spread new ideas. Some of these new ideas were about religion. During the **Reformation**, some Christian thinkers rejected the practices of the Catholic Church. These Protestants called for people to have more control over their religious affairs. Wars between Catholic and Protestant political leaders began over these debates.

Expansion and Imperialism

In 1492, Christopher Columbus sailed west across the Atlantic Ocean. He was trying to reach Asia. Instead, he landed in the Americas. More Europeans followed. Europeans set up new empires in the Americas. They brought back crops that helped Europeans eat better. They also set up a long-distance slave trade.

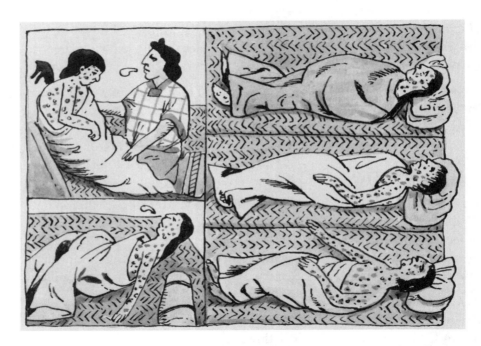

This illustration gives an Aztec view of the smallpox epidemic. What does it suggest about the Aztec's view of these events?

Thinkers around Europe began relying on reason again. Scientists of the 1500s and 1600s based their views on observations and experiments. This led to a **Scientific Revolution,** in which scientists challenged old ideas about the world. They determined that Earth orbited the Sun, for example. In the 1700s, interest in reason led to the **Enlightenment**. Enlightenment philosophers argued that people had natural human rights. These ideas helped inspire revolutions in the United States and France.

European countries lost power in the Americas. In the 1800s, however, they conquered lands and set up new colonies in Africa and Asia. This policy was known as **imperialism**. It helped keep Great Britain, France, and Germany strong. But it often went against the interests of people living under colonial rule.

Connect to Today

The Magna Carta was written centuries ago, but its ideas influence modern U.S. practices. For example, the Magna Carta established the idea that the king was subject to laws. It stated that all citizens had the right to equal treatment under the law. It also gave people accused of crimes the right to a trial.

Complete the activities below to check your understanding of the lesson content. The Unit 1 Answer Key is on page 150.

Vocabulary

Write definitions in your own words for each of the key terms.

1. democracy _____

2. imperialism _____

3. Renaissance _____

4. Scientific Revolution _____

Apply Your Knowledge

Add the number for each of the events below to the timeline to show the correct sequence of events.

5. Roman Empire collapses

6. European nations colonize Africa

7. Magna Carta is signed

8. Alexander the Great conquers many lands

9. Farming begins in Mesopotamia

10. Christopher Columbus arrives in the Americas

Skills Practice

Read the paragraph from the lesson. Then choose the correct answer to each question.

Thinkers around Europe began relying on reason again. Scientists of the 1500s and 1600s based their views on observations and experiments. This led to a Scientific Revolution, in which scientists challenged old ideas about the world. They determined that Earth orbited the Sun, for example. In the 1700s, interest in reason led to the Enlightenment. Enlightenment philosophers argued that people had natural human rights. These ideas helped inspire revolutions in the United States and France.

11. Which sentence from this paragraph gives its central idea?

   A. Thinkers around Europe began relying on reason again.

   B. They determined that Earth orbited the Sun, for example.

   C. In the 1700s, interest in reason led to the Enlightenment.

   D. These ideas helped inspire revolutions in the United States and France.

12. Which detail could be added to the paragraph to support its central idea?

   A. Many scientists lived in Northern Europe instead of in Italy.

   B. This was called the heliocentric model of the solar system.

   C. The Enlightenment led people to think critically about their rulers.

   D. George Washington became the first president of the United States.

TURNING POINTS IN WORLD HISTORY—THE EAST

Key Terms

communism

cultural diffusion

dynasty

Quran

Silk Roads

Connect to Today

Islam is the world's second largest religion today. More than 1.6 billion people worldwide are Muslims. One 2015 report said that Islam may become the world's largest religion by 2100. Some parts of the world already have huge Islamic majorities. The Middle East, parts of Africa, and parts of Southeast Asia are all populated mostly by Muslims.

Powerful civilizations also emerged in the Eastern Hemisphere. Major empires covered the Middle East, India, and China. Trade connected Africa, Asia, and Europe.

Ancient China and India

People began farming independently in Asia by about 5000 BCE. Early Chinese governments known as **dynasties** formed by 2000 BCE. These dynasties passed power through ruling families. China was ruled by many dynasties over time.

The Chinese were skilled at technology. Under the earliest dynasties the Chinese learned to work with bronze and iron. They later developed writing and paper. Chinese weavers made silk fabrics. The Chinese also developed gunpowder. After about 500 BCE, Chinese thinkers formed belief systems like Confucianism and Daoism. All of these spread through trade and **cultural diffusion**. Cultural diffusion is the movement of ideas and beliefs.

Societies also formed in India. Rulers formed powerful ancient empires there. Some early emperors helped spread religions like Hinduism and Buddhism throughout the region. They also supported science and mathematics. Indian scholars first developed the modern number system.

Founding and Spread of Islam

The prophet Muhammad founded the religion of Islam in the mid-600s CE. Islam combines elements of older religions such as Judaism and Christianity. Its main teachings are collected in the Muslim holy book called the **Quran**. After Muhammad died, Muslims disagreed about who should lead the faith. At this time, most Muslims formed a sect known as Sunni Islam. A minority formed a competing sect called Shia Islam.

Conquerors and missionaries expanded Islam's influence. Several powerful empires in the Middle East and Asia adopted Islam. The Mughal Empire encouraged Islam in India. In the West, Muslims called Moors gained control of Spain. Muslim scholars advanced science and kept Greek knowledge alive.

Traders also spread Islam throughout the Middle East and North Africa. In West Africa, powerful kingdoms ruled from about 750 CE to about 1600 CE. These kingdoms became rich by trading gold and salt. West African cities like Timbuktu were centers of Muslim culture and learning.

New Empires

During the 1200s, nomadic warriors from Central Asia conquered huge amounts of land. The Mongol Empire stretched from China to the Middle East. It even included much of Russia. The Mongols kept roads and provinces safe. This encouraged the growth of trade. Important trade routes known as the **Silk Roads** connected Asia to the Mediterranean during this time.

Part of the Roman Empire had split off in the 300s CE. It had a separate ruler and government with a capital at Constantinople. This government became the Byzantine Empire, which ruled over much of the Eastern Mediterranean. Turkish warriors known as the Ottomans captured Constantinople in 1453. The Byzantine Empire fell, and the Ottoman Empire took its place.

The Ottoman Empire kept the capital at Constantinople but changed its name to Istanbul. The empire was very powerful. It controlled lands from Greece to North Africa to the Middle East. The Ottomans helped spread Islam throughout their empire. The Ottoman Empire lasted until the 1920s.

Changes in East and South Asia

For many years, Great Britain ruled over India. An Indian independence movement formed. In 1947, Great Britain gave the nation independence. Britain also divided India into two countries, India and Pakistan. This led to conflict and violence. Despite these troubles, India inspired other nations to work for independence. Countries all around Asia successfully gained independence during the mid-1900s. Today, India is the world's largest democracy.

China also underwent political changes in the 1940s. A communist government gained power there in 1949. Under **communism**, resources are owned by everyone and managed by the state. China struggled for many decades. By the late 1900s, the Chinese government started to loosen economic rules. China became one of the world's most powerful economies. But people worry that its government treats citizens too harshly.

Skills Tip

Historians look closely at the relationships among events. One common relationship is cause-and-effect. A cause is an event that makes another event happen. An effect is a result. Events may have more than one cause or more than one effect. To help find cause-and-effect, look for clue words like *because, since,* and *led to.* Find the sentence *This led to conflict and violence.* What was the cause of this event?

French activists protest Chinese actions against a native ethnic group.

Complete the activities below to check your understanding of the lesson content. The Unit 1 Answer Key is on page 150.

Vocabulary

Complete each sentence with a key term from the lesson.

1. Muslims today follow teachings from the _____, which was written by Muhammad.

2. The growth of civilizations in China led ruling _____ to form there.

3. Under _____, government closely manages the economy.

4. Trade and migration are two main ways that _____ takes place.

Apply Your Knowledge

Choose the correct answer to each question.

5. Ancient Indian scholars developed

    A. gunpowder.

    B. numerals.

    C. paper.

    D. silk.

6. Which of these were most important to ancient West African kingdoms?

    A. books and writing

    B. iron and gunpowder

    C. silk and bronze

    D. gold and salt

Skills Practice

Match each cause with the correct effect. One cause has two effects.

Causes

7. The Mongol Empire began.

8. The Ottoman Empire began.

9. Great Britain ended its control of India.

Effects

A. Constantinople became Istanbul.

B. Asian countries sought independence.

C. Islam spread far and wide.

D. Trade on the Silk Roads grew.

Answer the questions based on the content covered in this unit. The Unit 1 Answer Key is on page 151.

1. Add each characteristic to the correct box in the table.

Functional Region	Perceptual Region

A. vary based on a person's ideas

B. usually centered on a city

C. are not used formally

D. typical of metropolitan areas

E. have often-changing boundaries

F. may be administered as a political unit

2. A geographer wishes to determine the extent to which a country's population is likely to grow or decline. Along the birth rate and death rate, what piece of information would best help her analysis?

A. population of largest city

B. climate zone assignment

C. gross domestic product

D. annual immigration rate

Use this excerpt from a 2015 speech by President Barack Obama to answer questions 3 and 4.

The science is indisputable. The fossil fuels we burn release carbon dioxide, which traps heat. And the levels of carbon dioxide in the atmosphere are now higher than they have been in 800,000 years. The planet is getting warmer. Fourteen of the 15 hottest years on record have been in the past 15 years. Last year was the planet's warmest year ever recorded.

Our scientists at NASA just reported that some of the sea ice around Antarctica is breaking up even faster than expected. The world's glaciers are melting, pouring new water into the ocean. Over the past century, the world sea level rose by about eight inches. That was in the last century; by the end of this century, it's projected to rise another one to four feet. . . .

And this is not just a problem for countries on the coasts or for certain regions of the world. Climate change will impact every country on the planet. No nation is immune. So, I'm here today to say that climate change constitutes a serious threat to global security, an immediate risk to our national security. And make no mistake, it will impact how our military defends our country. And so we need to act—and we need to act now.

3. Based on the excerpt, which policy would President Obama most likely support to address the problems he identifies?

A. increased support for data collection and analysis by NASA

B. recruitment of more soldiers to defend the nation's resources

C. passage of rules requiring factories to release less carbon dioxide

D. shift in government funding from oil to coal exploration

4. Which statement from the excerpt gives an opinion?

A. The fossil fuels we burn release carbon dioxide, which traps heat.

B. Fourteen of the 15 hottest years on record have been in the past 15 years.

C. That was in the last century . . . one to four feet.

D. So I'm here today to say . . . immediate risk to our national security.

Refer to the map below to answer question 5.

U.S. Climate Regions

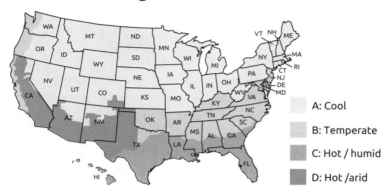

A: Cool

B: Temperate

C: Hot / humid

D: Hot /arid

5. Much of Northern Africa has a hot, dry climate that is inhospitable to agriculture and settlement. Which U.S. zone has a climate most similar to this region of North Africa?

    A. Zone A

    B. Zone B

    C. Zone C

    D. Zone D

Refer to the table below to answer questions 6–8.

Average High and Low Temperatures in F°, Los Angeles, CA												
	Jan	**Feb**	**Mar**	**Apr**	**May**	**Jun**	**Jul**	**Aug**	**Sept**	**Oct**	**Nov**	**Dec**
High	68	69	70	73	74	78	83	84	83	79	73	68
Low	48	49	51	54	57	60	64	64	63	59	52	47

6. The average high temperature in Los Angeles for the months of July through December is _____ degrees F.

7. The median low temperature in Los Angeles for the entire year is _____ degrees F.

8. The mode of low temperatures in Los Angeles for the entire year is _____ degrees F.

9. Which of these are examples of city-states?

    A. Athens and Sparta

    B. Missouri and California

    C. India and China

    D. Rome and Constantinople

10. How did ancient Greek civilization most influence modern U.S. society?

    A. It inspired artists of the Renaissance era.

    B. It established the philosophy of natural rights.

    C. It developed the first democratic government.

    D. It relied on a system of self-governing cities

11. The development of ancient Chinese and Indian civilizations was most similar in that they both

    A. relied on democratic systems of government.

    B. sought to imitate the culture of ancient Rome.

    C. adapted ideas introduced by cultural diffusion.

    D. established Islam as an official state religion.

U.S. History

Native Americans settled across America before European colonists arrived. In time, colonists became independent. The United States grew quickly. It spread toward the Pacific Ocean. Americans disagreed over important issues. They fought to end slavery and expand rights. They made technological discoveries. They fought in wars and chose leaders. Like you, people in the past read books, listened to music, and had families. American history is often seen as the story of progress.

All these past events influence your own life. Americans enjoy rights because people in the past worked for them. They also must solve problems caused by decisions made in the past. In the future, Americans will live in the world we create today.

The 1872 painting *American Progress,* by John Gast, expressed many Americans' desire to move West and establish new communities there.

Unit 2 Lesson 1 — THE AMERICAS BEFORE 1492

History includes all the people, events, and ideas that have ever happened. It studies how the decisions made at one time affect events that happen later. Historians also think about how people relate to one another. They discuss how changes and similarities over time shape our world.

Settlement of the Americas

Historians do not all agree about how people first came to the Americas. One common theory is that **hunter-gatherers** crossed from Asia to North America. Hunter-gatherers are people who survive by hunting wild animals and collecting edible plants.

Key Terms

adobe

Aztec

hunter-gatherer

Inca

Iroquois Confederacy

irrigation

Maya

Mesoamerica

Vocabulary Tip

Historians use several different words to describe groups of people in the past. These often relate to how they raised food. Pastoralists are people who herded animals, such as sheep. Pastoralists were nomads, which means they traveled from place to place. Agriculturalists are people who raised crops. They mostly lived in communities.

About 20,000 years ago, a narrow strip of land existed near what is now Alaska. People likely crossed this land and slowly spread southward. They may also have crossed the ocean in small boats, stopping at islands along the way.

People were living in the Americas as early as 13,000 years ago. They survived as hunter-gatherers for thousands of years. By about 6,000 BCE, early Native Americans had begun to farm. As in other places, they built complex societies as food surpluses grew.

Civilizations in North America

Many groups in North America were farmers. Northeastern people like the Iroquois and Algonquin grew crops and fished. They usually lived in small villages. The Iroquois formed a league known as the **Iroquois Confederacy**. Members agreed to make decisions together and protect one another during wartime.

People across the Great Plains also farmed. One important culture in this region was the Mississippian. Mississippians built a city at Cahokia, in what is now western Illinois. As many as 40,000 people lived in Cahokia.

The Southwest was very dry, but Native Americans there also farmed. They built **irrigation** systems to carry water to their crops. One main group in the Southwest was the Pueblo. They are named for the large buildings they constructed from dried mud bricks, which are called **adobe** bricks.

The Pueblo built settlements with large buildings made of adobe bricks.

Civilizations in Mesoamerica and South America

Mesoamerica included what is now Mexico and Central America. Mesoamerican civilizations were often strong and powerful. The **Maya** of northeastern Mexico and Guatemala built cities centered on huge temples and public buildings. They had advanced skills in architecture and astronomy. As the Maya declined, the Toltec and later **Aztec** became powerful. They built a city at Tenochtitlan and ruled a large empire.

The most powerful civilization in South America was the **Inca.** The Inca had an empire along the western coast of South America. They built an extensive road system to oversee the empire and conduct trade. They also built cities, wrote laws, and developed advanced metalworking technology.

Skills Tip

Historians may study the past by analyzing photos or illustrations created by people who lived long ago. To help yourself analyze an image, begin by asking questions like these: *Who created this image? What does it show? Why was it made?*

The Inca created richly detailed ornaments like this one.

LESSON REVIEW

Complete the activities below to check your understanding of the lesson content. The Unit 2 Answer Key is on page 151.

Vocabulary

Write definitions in your own words for each of the key terms.

1. adobe _____

   _____

2. hunter-gatherer _____

   _____

3. irrigation _____

   _____

4. Mesoamerica _____

   _____

Complete each sentence with a key term from the lesson.

5. The _____ built many good roads across parts of South America.

6. Scholars of the _____ studied astronomy and architecture to build large pyramids.

Skills Practice

Study the illustration. Then write complete sentences to answer the questions that follow.

7. Who do you think created this illustration?

    _____

    _____

8. What main topic does this illustration show?

    _____

    _____

9. What is one detail that tells about this illustration's topic?

    _____

    _____

10. Why do you think this illustration was created?

    _____

    _____

A few Europeans had reached the Americas before 1492. Two regions developed separately. All that changed after Christopher Columbus arrived.

Journeying Westward

During the 1400s, Europeans began actively exploring the world. Prince Henry the Navigator of Portugal sponsored trips to West Africa. Their success encouraged the Portuguese and others to sail farther. Improved technology also helped spur exploration. A new type of ship called the **caravel** was light and fast. Navigation tools helped sailors find their position far out at sea and stay on course.

Europeans wished to find a water route to Asia, which had many valuable trade goods. In the 1480s, Portuguese explorer Bartolomeu Dias sailed all the way to South Africa. Italian navigator Christopher Columbus thought a shorter route was possible by sailing west. He convinced the Spanish king and queen to fund his voyage. In 1492, Columbus landed in the Caribbean. He returned to Spain with stories of riches. Columbus made several more journeys to the Americas. His efforts inspired other Europeans to sail west.

Results of European Contact

Millions of people lived across the Americas in 1492. But small groups of Europeans easily conquered them. The Spanish and Portuguese had important advantages. They rode horses, which did not live in the Americas. They had sharp steel swords and strong armor. Europeans also introduced devastating diseases such as **smallpox**. Smallpox infected and killed huge numbers of native people. The movement of plants, animals, and diseases during this time is called the **Columbian Exchange**.

European conquerors enslaved native people. They forced them to grow crops and work in silver mines. As native people died from disease or harsh treatment, Europeans looked for a new source of labor. They began importing slaves from West Africa. West African warlords kidnapped people and sold them to Europeans. European ships transported Africans across the **Middle Passage**. This long journey across the Atlantic was extremely difficult. People were crammed onto ships with poor sanitation. Many died on the voyage. Those who survived were often enslaved in the Caribbean.

Key Terms

caravel

cash crop

Columbian Exchange

Mayflower Compact

Middle Colonies

Middle Passage

New England

plantation

smallpox

Southern Colonies

Skills Tip

Historical texts often retell events in sequence. As you read, look for words like *first, then, next,* and *later* to help show sequence. Look, too, for specific dates when events happened. Finding and analyzing sequence can help you better understand the connections among events. Reread the text under *Journeying Westward.* In what sequence did Dias and Columbus complete their voyages? How can you tell?

EUROPEAN COLONIZATION

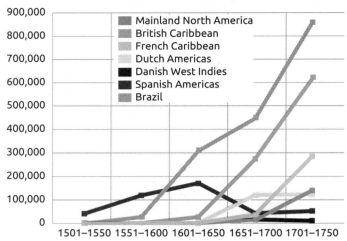

Slaves Arriving in the Americas, 1501–1750

Legend:
- Mainland North America
- British Caribbean
- French Caribbean
- Dutch Americas
- Danish West Indies
- Spanish Americas
- Brazil

Source: Emory University, Trans-Atlantic Slave Trade Database

Notice the patterns of slaves arriving in different regions of the Americas over time. Which region had the most arrivals? Which had the fewest?

New England

New England included the colonies in the far northeast of what is today the United States. The Pilgrims were the first European group to settle permanently in New England. They were a religious group who wished to separate from the Church of England. The English king opposed the Pilgrims. In 1620, a group of Pilgrims and others sailed from England on the Mayflower. Before they landed in Plymouth, Massachusetts, leaders signed the **Mayflower Compact**. This document agreed that everyone on the ship would settle together and manage their affairs. It was the first framework of government in America.

Over time, other important settlements grew up in New England. The largest one was Boston. People who disagreed with the Pilgrims' religious rules set up colonies in Rhode Island and Connecticut.

New England's climate was cold, and the land was hard to farm. People relied on fishing, logging, and trade to supplement their crops. As a result, many New Englanders lived in villages and small towns.

Middle Colonies

The **Middle Colonies** lie to the south of New England. This region had a warmer climate and a long coastline. It became the colonial breadbasket, growing wheat and other crops for trade with other colonial regions.

The colonies of this region were very diverse. William Penn was an English Quaker who wanted to form a colony that practiced religious toleration. Pennsylvania welcomed Quakers, Catholics, Anglicans, and others. Maryland was founded as a Catholic colony. Dutch settlers founded the city of New Amsterdam. It was conquered by the English and renamed New York. Along with Philadelphia, it was an important hub of trade and commerce.

Southern Colonies

The **Southern Colonies** reached from Virginia southward to the border with Spanish Florida. The Southern Colonies were more sparsely settled than New England or the Middle Colonies. People lived on large farms called **plantations** or smaller family farms across the countryside. They grew **cash crops** like rice and tobacco. They then sold these crops for profit. The Southern Colonies had just one important city at Charleston, South Carolina.

Slaves did much of the work on plantations. In the early 1700s, South Carolina had more enslaved African Americans than free white residents. When Georgia was founded in 1732, it banned slavery. Its founder hoped to limit the growth of plantations. But it, too, came to allow slavery after coming under the power of the English king.

The importance of slavery in the Southern Colonies set them apart from the rest of America. Many more slaves lived in the South than elsewhere. Southerners relied on slaves to run their economy. This system caused serious problems after the founding of the United States.

Connect to Today

Regions formed during the colonial era continue to shape how people see the United States today. Recall the U.S. regions you learned about in Unit 1. New England is one sub-region of what is now the Northeast. The Southern colonies form part of the modern South. People in these places are still influenced by the cultures and economy set up during colonial times.

Colonial Regions

Geography shaped life in each of the three colonial regions.

Complete the activities below to check your understanding of the lesson content. The Unit 2 Answer Key is on page 151.

Vocabulary

Choose the correct answer to each question.

1. Which of the following was a major colonial cash crop?

   A. squash

   B. timber

   C. wheat

   D. rice

2. Why did people travel on the Middle Passage?

   A. They were forced to go as slaves.

   B. They hoped to find riches and adventures.

   C. They were part of Christopher Columbus's crew.

   D. They wanted to escape religious persecution.

Apply Your Knowledge

Label each characteristic as belonging to New England, the Middle Colonies, or the Southern Colonies.

3. religious diversity _____

4. many cash crops _____

5. relied heavily on slavery _____

6. settled by Pilgrims _____

7. logging and fishing _____

8. colonial breadbasket _____

Skills Practice

Read the text. Then add four events from the text to the timeline in the correct sequence.

Anne Hutchinson helped found the colony of Rhode Island. She was born in England in 1591. Later, she settled in Boston, Massachusetts, with her husband. She gave speeches and talks there about religion. Her actions angered Boston's leaders. They expelled her from the colony in 1638. Soon after, she and some followers founded a new settlement in what is now Portsmouth, Rhode Island.

9.

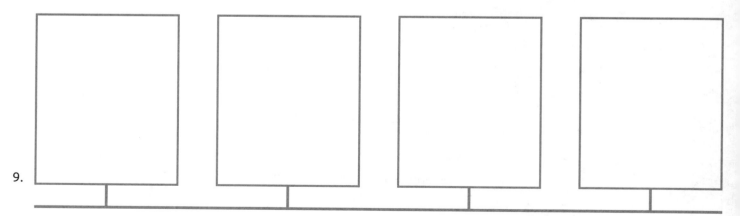

French and Indian War

Great Britain controlled colonies across eastern North America. Americans thought of themselves as British citizens. But events made them wish to become independent.

Great Britain claimed all of the land of the American colonies. France and Spain also had large land claims in North America. Native Americans also wanted to keep rights to the lands where they already lived. Several wars over territory happened during the colonial era. The **French and Indian War** was the largest and most important.

By the 1750s, British settlers wanted to move farther west. They wanted to claim lands in what in now western Pennsylvania, Ohio, and Michigan. The French and their Native American allies resisted this push. Fighting between British and French armies over the land began in 1754. It continued for nine years. At first, it seemed like the French were stronger. But the British and American troops eventually won. France gave up a great deal of land as a result of the war. Great Britain gained control of Canada. Spain took over the Louisiana Territory. Spain kept control of it until 1800, when it gave the Louisiana Territory back to France.

The British king wished to avoid another war with Native Americans. He issued the **Proclamation of 1763** to set a limit on westward expansion. But many American settlers ignored the proclamation. They believed they had a right to settle on western lands.

Declaring Independence

Fighting the French and Indian War was very expensive. The British government thought the colonists should help pay its war debts. It passed several new taxes on the colonies after the war. The Stamp Act was a tax on printed materials. The Tea Act made colonists pay a tax on imported tea. The Sugar Act taxed imported sugar and molasses. These taxes and others angered the colonists. They thought the taxes were unfair. Colonists could not vote for representatives in **Parliament**. Parliament is the British law-making body.

Some colonists actively resisted British laws. In 1773, colonists dressed as Native Americans dumped tea into Boston Harbor. This was known as the Boston Tea Party. Other colonists gave speeches and wrote pamphlets. Thomas Paine wrote a pamphlet called *Common Sense*. It encouraged Americans to demand independence.

Key Terms

boycott

Declaration of Independence

French and Indian War

Loyalist

Parliament

Proclamation of 1763

Treaty of Paris

Skills Tip

Texts can contain both facts and opinions. A fact is a statement that can be proven true. An opinion is a statement that tells the ideas of the author. Read these two sentences: *These taxes and others angered the colonists. They thought the taxes were unfair.* These are both facts because they can be proven with sources. Now read these two sentences: *These taxes and others angered the colonists. The taxes were unfair.* The second statement now gives an opinion. Colonists and the British government disagreed about whether the taxes were fair or unfair. Therefore, the statement cannot be proven.

An artist's rendering of the Boston Tea Party

Leaders from different colonies gathered at a Continental Congress in 1774. They decided the colonies should **boycott** British goods. A boycott is a refusal to buy or use something. The situation got worse. Fighting between colonists and the British began in 1775. Another Continental Congress gathered soon after. This time, leaders decided to name George Washington the head of the colonial troops. These troops were called the Continental Army. The leaders also decided to officially declare independence. Thomas Jefferson wrote the **Declaration of Independence**. It was adopted in 1776.

Fighting for Freedom

Led by George Washington, the Continental Army fought in the American Revolution to overcome well-trained British troops. Many problems worried the colonial army. Colonists lost many battles early in the war. They had little training and few supplies. But they fought for a cause they believed in. A turning point came in 1777. Americans won at the Battles of Saratoga. This convinced France to give the colonists military aid. The colonists began to triumph. American and French forces finally defeated the British in 1781 at the Battle of Yorktown. Britain surrendered. Great Britain and the United States signed the **Treaty of Paris** in 1783. This officially gave the United States independence.

Not all colonists fought for independence. **Loyalists** supported the British government. They thought the rebellion was a crime. Some Loyalists worked for the British crown. Others opposed war in general. The number of Loyalists varied from place to place.

Complete the activities below to check your understanding of the lesson content. The Unit 2 Answer Key is on page 151.

Vocabulary

Match each key term with its definition.

1. French and Indian War
2. Parliament
3. Declaration of Independence
4. Proclamation of 1763
5. boycott
6. Treaty of Paris

A. British lawmaking body

B. document limiting western settlement

C. conflict fought from 1754 to 1763

D. agreement officially giving the United States independence

E. document announcing colonial independence

F. refusal to buy or use goods

Skills Practice

Read the paragraph from Common Sense *by Thomas Paine. Then choose the correct answer to each question.*

No country on the globe is so happily situated, or so internally capable of raising a fleet as America. Tar, timber, iron, and cordage are her natural produce. We need go abroad for nothing. Whereas the Dutch, who make large profits by hiring out their ships of war to the Spaniards and Portuguese, are obliged to import most of their materials they use. We ought to view the building a fleet as an article of commerce, it being the natural manufactory of this country. It is the best money we can lay out. A navy when finished is worth more than it cost. And is that nice point in national policy, in which commerce and protection are united. Let us build; if we want them not, we can sell; and by that means replace our paper currency with ready gold and silver.

7. Which sentence from the excerpt gives a fact?

   A. No country on the . . . as America.

   B. Tar, timber . . . are her natural produce.

   C. It is the best money we can lay out.

   D. A navy when finished is worth more than it cost.

8. Which of the following people would most likely disagree with the opinions presented in this text?

   A. a participant in the Boston Tea Party

   B. a delegate to the Continental Congress

   C. a Loyalist from New York

   D. a member of George Washington's army

Key Terms

administration

Articles of Confederation

Bill of Rights

Cabinet

constitution

Great Compromise

Northwest Ordinance

ratify

Three-Fifths Compromise

Skills Tip

When reading, look for specific evidence to support or weaken a text's main claims. These details help show how an author builds his or her argument. For example, this text states *People soon began to think that the Articles could not last for long.* Notice that the next sentence in the paragraph gives a piece of evidence to support that main claim: *A rebellion led by Daniel Shays in Massachusetts highlighted its weaknesses.*

Articles of Confederation

The Continental Congress governed the colonies during the American Revolution. After fighting ended in 1781, Americans needed to create a more lasting system. It took them almost 20 years to form the government we know today.

The nation's first plan for government was the **Articles of Confederation**. The Articles took effect in 1781. They organized the states under a loose, weak national government. This government had just one political body—the Congress. Each state sent delegates to the Congress. Congress had some powers. For example, it could make foreign policy and oversee wars. It could run a postal service. It could also borrow money. But it lacked the power to make states follow its wishes.

The main achievement of the U.S. government during this time was the passage of the **Northwest Ordinance**. These laws organized what was then the West into territories. The Northwest Ordinance set up a system to measure and lay out the land into districts called townships. It explained how territories could apply to become states. It also banned slavery all throughout the Northwest Territory. States like Ohio and Indiana were organized under this plan.

People soon began to think that the Articles could not last for long. A rebellion led by Daniel Shays in Massachusetts highlighted its weaknesses. Leaders argued that the United States needed a stronger national government to solve its problems.

The troubles of Shays' Rebellion showed the weakness of the central U.S. government.

Writing the Constitution

Political leaders from all over the United States gathered in Philadelphia in 1787. They planned to revise the Articles of Confederation. But they soon decided to simply start over with a new plan for the U.S. government. This plan is known as the **Constitution**. The delegates chose George Washington to lead the meeting.

The delegates agreed to make the national government stronger. They set up a federal system with two levels of power. The national, or federal, government kept some powers. The states kept others. Some powers were shared. They also agreed to set up three separate branches of government. One branch held the Congress. Another was led by a president. The third included a Supreme Court.

Delegates disagreed on many decisions, however. One main split was between small states and large states. Small states wanted to have a voice in the national government. Large states believed that they deserved more say because they had more people. This resulted in the **Great Compromise**. Under the Great Compromise, Congress had two houses. The House of Representatives had membership based on population. This gave large states a greater voice. The Senate had two members per state no matter its population. This gave small states an equal voice.

Another major problem was slavery. Some Northern states had already begun to end slavery. Southern states wished to protect it in the Constitution. The Constitution had two main compromises about slavery. First, it stated that the Congress could not discuss the slave trade for 20 years. This meant it was protected for at least that time. Second, it agreed that states could count each slave as three-fifths of a person when setting the number of representatives. The **Three-Fifths Compromise** gave Southern states with many slaves a bigger voice in government, even though those people were not truly represented by their leaders.

Many of America's most-respected thinkers and political leaders helped write the U.S. Constitution.

Vocabulary Tip

When it is in written with a lowercase letter, a *constitution* is any plan for government. The *U.S. Constitution* is the plan for government just for the United States. Usually, it is written as *the Constitution*.

Ratifying the Constitution

State legislatures debated whether to **ratify,** or agree to, the new plan. Some agreed quickly. They believed the Constitution was sound. Others worried it did not do enough to protect people from a strong government. People remembered the American Revolution. They wanted to keep the new government from being too much like the British government.

James Madison, Alexander Hamilton, and John Jay all contributed to a series of essays supporting the new plan. They wrote under a shared pen name, Publius. The essays were mostly collected in a book called *The Federalist*. They argue for the federal system. They also pointed out the problems of the old government.

Some states were still reluctant. They wanted some changes made to the Constitution to protect certain rights. National leaders agreed to add amendments protecting individual and state rights. This led enough states to ratify the Constitution that it went into effect in 1789. Congress then sent twelve amendments to the states for approval. Ten were added to the Constitution in 1791. These ten are called the **Bill of Rights**.

U.S. Government Begins

In 1789, George Washington became the first U.S. president. His **administration,** or government, set up processes still used today. For example, Washington named advisers to a **Cabinet**. These advisers helped him make decisions.

Washington hoped U.S. politics would remain free from the influence of interest groups and political parties. But disagreements over issues split leaders into groups called factions. One main issue was over the nation's finances. One faction wished to create a national bank. This bank could help manage the debts from the American Revolution and issue money. Alexander Hamilton led this faction. Another faction, led by Thomas Jefferson, opposed this plan. They thought it was unconstitutional. Over time, these factions became the first political parties.

Complete the activities below to check your understanding of the lesson content. The Unit 2 Answer Key is on page 151.

Vocabulary

Complete each sentence with a key term from the lesson.

1. The _____ were adopted in 1781 as the first U.S. plan for government.

2. Congress added the _____ to the U.S. Constitution to protect certain individual and state freedoms.

3. George Washington created a _____ to give him advice about important decisions.

4. Territories like Ohio and Indiana were organized under laws called the _____.

Skills Practice

Read the excerpt from Federalist No. 10. *(A faction is a group within a larger group that has different ideas and opinions than the rest of the group.) Then write complete sentences to answer the questions that follow.*

There are again two methods of removing the causes of faction: the one, by destroying the liberty which is essential to its existence; the other, by giving to every citizen the same opinions, the same passions, and the same interests.

It could never be more truly said than of the first remedy, that it was worse than the disease. Liberty is to faction what air is to fire, an ailment without which it instantly expires. But it could not be less folly to abolish liberty, which is essential to political life, because it nourishes faction, than it would be to wish the annihilation of air, which is essential to animal life, because it imparts to fire its destructive agency.

5. Based on this excerpt, what opinion does the author have about factions?

_____

_____

6. What main claim does the author make in Paragraph 1?

_____

_____

7. What main claim does the author make in Paragraph 2?

_____

_____

8. What is one piece of evidence from the text to support this claim? Explain what the evidence says.

_____

_____

In 1845, a newspaper editor wrote that it was the nation's "**manifest destiny**" to expand to the Pacific Ocean. This idea captured the spirit of the era.

Growing the Nation

In 1803, French leader Napoleon Bonaparte unexpectedly offered to sell the United States a huge amount of land in North America. President Thomas Jefferson was not certain he had the right, under the U.S. Constitution, to buy the land. But he was eager to grow the nation's territory westward. He also wanted to make sure Americans had access to the Mississippi River. The river was an important shipping route. The United States quickly agreed to buy the land from France. This land became known as the **Louisiana Purchase**. It grew U.S. lands from New Orleans all the way to what is now Montana. The new Louisiana Territory doubled the nation's size.

The Louisiana Purchase grew national interest in expanding even more. Americans soon took control of Florida. People streamed into Western lands. Mexico and Great Britain claimed these lands, however, and Native Americans already lived there. Some American immigrants in Texas led a war for independence from Mexico in the 1830s. Texas soon joined the United States. Great Britain agreed to U.S. claims in the Pacific Northwest in 1846. Two years later, the nation gained huge territories in the West. Mexico gave up these lands in the **Treaty of Guadalupe-Hidalgo,** ending the Mexican-American War.

At the same time, better technology helped the nation. The government and private companies built canals. Later, they built railroads. These moved goods and people faster and cheaper than had been possible before. The development of standardized interchangeable parts allowed goods to be made in factories. Industrialization took hold, mostly in the Northeast.

Debate Over Slavery

National growth caused trouble over slavery. Northern states had started abolishing slavery in the late 1700s. They usually emancipated enslaved people over time. **Emancipate** means to set free. The Southern economy and society, however, relied heavily on slavery. The invention of the cotton gin made growing cotton very profitable. The cotton gin was a machine that cleaned cotton plants. During the early 1800s, cotton became the region's most important cash crop. People called it "king cotton."

Southern plantation owners used lots of enslaved laborers to plant, tend, and harvest cotton plants. Southerners also owned slaves to grow other crops, tend to household duties, and perform all kinds of jobs. Most Southerners could not afford to own slaves, but across the South people believed that slavery was central to their way of life. Some Northerners benefitted from slavery, too. "King cotton" was used in Northern textile factories and sold by Northern merchants.

The North, however, was turning to manufacturing. Its jobs and farmlands attracted immigrants from places like Germany and Ireland. A growing number of Northerners wanted slaves to be freed across the country. These people were called **abolitionists**. Most abolitionists thought slavery was morally wrong. Many believed it went against American ideals of democracy and liberty. Slaves often went through terrible treatment. They lacked nearly all rights.

Key Terms

abolitionist

emancipate

Fugitive Slave Act

Louisiana Purchase

manifest destiny

Missouri Compromise

popular sovereignty

sectionalism

Treaty of Guadalupe-Hidalgo

Connect to Today

Flags serve as important symbols. They stand for a place and its people. You probably already know, for example, that the U.S. flag has one star for each of its 50 states. It also has one stripe for each of the original 13 colonies. States also have flags. Some of these reflect major historical events. Texas's state flag is the one that was used by the independent Republic of Texas between 1835 and 1845. Likewise, California's state flag is inspired by the one flown by American settlers who rebelled against Mexican control of the territory there in 1846. They formed a short-lived "Bear Flag Republic" there.

Congress Compromises

The North and the South became more and more different. These differences led to the rise of **sectionalism**. Sectionalism is support for the needs of one's own region of the country, rather than to the country as a whole. Sectionalism contributed to growing tensions between the North and the South. U.S. leaders struggled to find ways to keep sectionalism from breaking the nation apart.

During the early 1800s, Northern and Southern politicians in the U.S. Congress agreed to certain policies. These policies tried to maintain the fragile balance between sectional interests. The **Missouri Compromise** of 1820 allowed Missouri to join the United States as a slave state. At the same time, Maine joined as a free state. This kept the number of slave and free states equal. The compromise also established a line running through the Louisiana Territory. No new states north of that line could allow slavery. But new states south of it could. Americans hoped the Missouri Compromise would settle the question of slavery for many years to come.

Skills Tip

A person's point of view includes the ideas and opinions that person has about a certain topic. Thinking about an author's point of view will help you to better understand a historical document. First, consider the author's historical context. What do you know about the author? When and where did he or she live? Then, consider what people at the time thought about the author or the topic of the document.

The Missouri Compromise, 1820

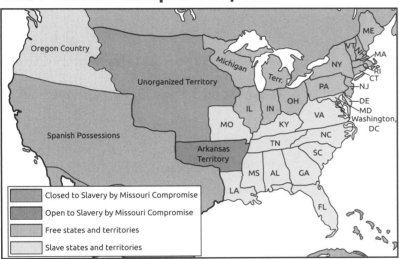

The Missouri Compromise organized the country. How might more expansion challenge this system of organization?

The nation continued to grow, however. The Missouri Compromise was not enough to prevent sectional tensions from rising again in the late 1840s. Congress passed a new series of laws known as the Compromise of 1850. This compromise let California enter the nation as a free state. It allowed people in the territories of New Mexico and Utah to vote on whether to allow slavery. This process is called **popular sovereignty**. The compromise also included a law called the **Fugitive Slave Act**. This law required people in all states—including free states—to help capture and return escaped slaves to their owners in the South. The Fugitive Slave Act angered people across the North. They thought it made them work to support slavery, even if they did not believe in it.

Complete the activities below to check your understanding of the lesson content. The Unit 2 Answer Key is on page 151.

Vocabulary

Write definitions in your own words for each of the key terms.

1. abolitionist _____

   _____

2. Louisiana Purchase _____

   _____

3. popular sovereignty _____

   _____

4. sectionalism _____

   _____

Complete each sentence with a key term from the lesson.

5. The U.S. Congress passed the _____ to set a line dividing future free states from slave states.

6. Americans believed it was the nation's _____ to expand all the way to the Pacific Ocean.

Skills Practice

Read the primary source document. Then write complete sentences to answer the questions that follow.

"Our manifest destiny [is] to overspread the continent allotted by Providence for the free development of our yearly multiplying millions. . . . [T]here is a great deal of Annexation yet to take place, within the life of the present generation, along the whole line of our northern border."

—John O'Sullivan, 1845

7. Who is the author of this document, and when was it written?

   _____

8. What did most Americans think about the subject of this document at the time it was written?

   _____

9. What point of view is the author giving in this document?

   _____

10. Who might have disagreed with the author's point of view? How might that person's or group's historical context have differed from the author's context?

    _____

    _____

    _____

A **civil war** is a war between groups within a country. The American Civil War was fought from 1861 to 1865. Historians believe that as many as 850,000 people died in the war.

Causes of the Civil War

During the mid-1800s, the United States was divided over slavery. Many people in the North opposed slavery. Abolitionists gave speeches and wrote books. Harriet Beecher Stowe wrote *Uncle Tom's Cabin*. It convinced many Northerners that slavery was wrong. But Southerners thought the Constitution protected slavery. They owned slaves as property. They argued that the Constitution included slaves in its guarantees of property rights. The South believed states, not the federal government, should decide laws about slavery. This idea was called **states' rights**.

Republican candidate Abraham Lincoln won the presidential election of 1860. Lincoln did not wish to abolish slavery. He did not want it to expand, however. Southerners worried Lincoln would end slavery altogether. South Carolina **seceded** soon after Lincoln's election. To secede is to leave a country. Other Southern states followed. Over time, 11 states left the Union. They formed the Confederate States of America.

Key Terms

civil war

Emancipation Proclamation

Freedmen's Bureau

Radical Republicans

Reconstruction

secede

states' rights

United States, 1861

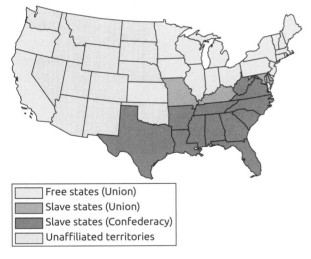

- ☐ Free states (Union)
- ☐ Slave states (Union)
- ☐ Slave states (Confederacy)
- ☐ Unaffiliated territories

A few states that allowed slavery stayed in the Union. These border states included Delaware, Maryland, Kentucky, and Missouri.

Fighting the War

The North and South each had advantages. The North had more industry and more people, so it could more easily make and move supplies. The South had good military generals, and its people believed in their cause. The South also did not need to win the war. It just needed to keep fighting until the North gave up.

Skills Tip

An inference is something that is suggested by an author. It is not directly stated. To make an inference, read the text carefully. Think about an idea that the details support but do not state. For example, read these two sentences: *Lee surrendered to Grant that April at Appomattox Courthouse. The war was over.* What can you infer from these details? *Appomattox Courthouse was the site of a final battle of the war.*

Connect to Today

The Fourteenth Amendment still causes controversy today. Some people dislike its citizenship clause. Anyone born in the United States is a citizen, even if his or her parents entered the country illegally or as tourists. Others think this is an important U.S. ideal. The Fourteenth Amendment has also caused major changes in U.S. laws. It was used to end the legal separation of the races. In 2015, the Supreme Court said it guaranteed same-sex couples the right to marry.

The South seemed likely to succeed at the beginning. It won battles and showed its commitment. But the tide slowly turned for the North. Lincoln issued the **Emancipation Proclamation** in January 1863. This freed all the slaves living in the Confederacy. It made Northerners believe winning the war would be a moral victory. Union troops won victories in the South that weakened Confederate supply lines. But the South fought on. It launched an attack in Union territory at Gettysburg, Pennsylvania. The Union won, and Lincoln gave a moving speech called the Gettysburg Address.

The North began to press harder. Ulysses S. Grant became head of the Union army in 1864. He led successful campaigns that weakened the South. General George T. Sherman destroyed land and farms across the Southeast. His troops burned Atlanta and Savannah. They freed slaves as they went. In 1865, Grant faced the skillful Southern general Robert E. Lee in Virginia. Lee surrendered to Grant that April at Appomattox Courthouse. The war was over.

Reconstruction

The United States needed to rebuild after the war ended. The states that had left the Union needed to rejoin. The war had destroyed land and buildings. It had also dramatically changed life in the South. The Emancipation Proclamation had freed some slaves, but slavery was still legal. The nation focused on these goals between 1865 and 1877. This time period is called **Reconstruction**.

Many leaders were angry at the South and wanted to punish them for the war. Lincoln hoped to take a more moderate path. However, he was assassinated soon after the war ended. Andrew Johnson became president. He wanted to treat the South gently. **Radical Republicans** in Congress opposed this plan. They put the South under military governors instead. During this time, former slaves won state and national political offices. The **Freedmen's Bureau** set up schools and helped former slaves find new work. Congress also passed three amendments protecting former slaves. They forced Southern states to ratify them to rejoin the Union.

Many Southerners disliked Reconstruction. Some groups organized to frighten African Americans. Reconstruction ended in 1877. The presidential election of 1876 did not have a clear winner. Historians believe the Republican president candidate, Rutherford B. Hayes, agreed to remove troops from the South. Some Southern delegates then supported him for president.

Reconstruction Amendments	
Amendment	**Purpose**
Thirteenth	Abolished slavery
Fourteenth	Extended citizenship to people of all races; guaranteed equal protection under the law
Fifteenth	Extended voting rights to people of all races

The Reconstruction Amendments made it unconstitutional to own slaves. They gave former slaves more rights.

Complete the activities below to check your understanding of the lesson content. The Unit 2 Answer Key is on page 151.

Skills Practice

Choose the correct answer to each question.

1. Radical Republicans were an important group in what?

    A. the Union Army

    B. the U.S. Congress

    C. the Confederate government

    D. the Freedmen's Bureau

2. What was an effect of the Emancipation Proclamation?

    A. Slavery was abolished in the United States.

    B. The Constitution was amended.

    C. Slaves in the South were legally freed.

    D. Some Southern states left the United States.

Apply Your Knowledge

3. Add each phrase below to the correct section of the graphic organizer.

Causes of the Civil War	Effects of the Civil War

new public schools

Thirteenth Amendment

idea of states' rights

disagreements over slavery

military governors in the South

election of Lincoln

Skills Practice

Read the excerpt from the Gettysburg Address. Then complete the activities that follow.

It is for us the living, rather, to be dedicated here to the unfinished work which they who fought here have thus far so nobly advanced. It is rather for us to be here dedicated to the great task remaining before us—that from these honored dead we take increased devotion to that cause for which they gave the last full measure of devotion—that we here highly resolve that these dead shall not have died in vain, that this nation under God shall have a new birth of freedom, and that government of the people, by the people, for the people, shall not perish from the earth.

4. Circle two main details from the text.

5. Write an inference that these two details support:

_____

INDUSTRIALIZATION AND REFORM

Key Terms

assembly line

assimilate

industrialization

initiative

Progressives

recall

referendum

Second Industrial Revolution

settlement house

telegraph

Transcontinental Railroad

urbanization

The nation changed greatly after the Civil War. Factories replaced farms. New Americans came from all over the world. Reformers tried to solve the problems of the new age.

Second Industrial Revolution

Before the Civil War, economic changes had begun in the Northeast. Factories that wove cotton into cloth opened. Machines did some of the work previously done by people. During the **Second Industrial Revolution,** these changes sped up. These changes, known as **industrialization,** happened during the late 1800s and early 1900s.

New technology spurred the Second Industrial Revolution. People discovered better ways to work with steel. This created a light and very strong building material. They learned to make better engines and refine oil into fuel. In the early 1900s, factories began making cars. Henry Ford owned the Ford Motor Company. He innovated a production process called the **assembly line.** Workers on an assembly line do the same job all day. Together, their efforts make a finished product. Assembly lines could produce more goods quickly and cheaply.

Transportation and communication also helped the Second Industrial Revolution. The **Transcontinental Railroad** linked the nation. It was made by building two rail lines toward one another. They met in Utah in 1869. Railroads allowed people to ship goods long distances. Refrigerated rail cars developed in the late 1870s allowed companies to ship meat. The **telegraph** sent messages quickly over long distances. By the late 1800s, some people also had telephones.

Ford's Model T cars on an assembly line, 1900

Immigration and Urbanization

Industrialization created new jobs and economic opportunity. People had long been immigrating to the United States. But millions more came in the late 1800s. Most new immigrants came from Southern and Eastern Europe. Four million people came from Italy alone between 1880 and 1920. Immigrants often settled in growing cities like New York and Chicago. They contributed to the growth of cities, known as **urbanization**.

Urbanization led to new challenges. So many people living close together helped spread diseases. Immigrants sometimes lived in small, cramped apartments without running water or sanitation. Fires and crime were both growing problems. Poor families sent children to work in factories instead of to attend school. Cities tried to meet these challenges. They set up new police and fire departments. Individuals and groups also tried to help. Jane Addams was a leader of the **settlement house** movement. She had a house in Chicago where immigrants could get help. They could take classes in English and other subjects, for example. Settlement houses tried to **assimilate**, or adapt, immigrants into U.S. society.

The Progressive Era

Industrialization and urbanization created new problems. Reformers called **Progressives** tried to fix those problems. They believed good government and laws could make a difference. Progressives included presidents like Theodore Roosevelt. They also included regular people working in their communities.

Progressives made important political changes. They introduced **recall, referendum, and initiative**. A recall is a vote to remove politicians from office. A referendum is a popular vote on a state law or amendment. An initiative is a ballot measure suggested by the people. Progressives also called for passage of federal laws for better food safety and other issues.

Skills Tip

A claim is a statement put forth in a text. For example, the statement *Most new immigrants came from Southern and Eastern Europe* is a claim. It gives information about immigration. How can you tell whether the author's claim is correct? Look closely at the evidence provided in the supporting details. The author states that *Four million people came from Italy alone between 1880 and 1920*. This statement gives a fact about where people came from to support the author's claim.

Complete the activities below to check your understanding of the lesson content. The Unit 2 Answer Key is on page 151.

Vocabulary

Write definitions in your own words for each of the key terms.

1. assimilate _____

    _____

2. initiative _____

    _____

3. settlement house _____

    _____

4. urbanization _____

    _____

Complete each sentence with a key term from the lesson.

5. The _____ linked the United States after its completion in 1869.

6. Progressive reformers began the _____ to remove corrupt or bad politicians from office.

Skills Practice

Read the paragraph from the lesson. Then choose the correct answer to each question.

Transportation and communication also helped the Second Industrial Revolution. The Transcontinental Railroad linked the nation. It was made by building two rail lines toward one another. They met in Utah in 1869. Railroads allowed people to ship goods long distances. Refrigerated rail cars developed in the late 1870s allowed companies to ship meat. The telegraph sent messages quickly over long distances. By the late 1800s, some people also had telephones.

7. Which sentence from the text gives the author's main claim?

    A. Transportation and communication also helped the Second Industrial Revolution.

    B. It was made by building two rail lines toward one another.

    C. Railroads allowed people to ship goods long distances.

    D. The telegraph sent messages quickly over long distances.

8. Which evidence from the text best supports the author's main claim?

    A. It was made by building two rail lines toward one another.

    B. They met in Utah in 1869.

    C. Refrigerated rail cars developed in the late 1870s allowed companies to ship meat.

    D. By the late 1800s, some people also had telephones.

A WORLD AT WAR

The world underwent great troubles during the early 1900s. Two world wars wracked the globe. Economic problems spread from the United States to Europe.

World War I

Europeans competed for power and influence during the early 1900s. Tensions among nations were very high. In 1914, a Serbian nationalist assassinated an Austrian duke. This started a chain reaction. Nations declared war on one another due to anger and military **alliances**. Alliances are agreements to work together. World War I began.

The war was unlike earlier wars. New weapons and tactics caused many **casualties,** or injuries and deaths. The conflict went on and on with no clear winner. Germany, Austria-Hungary, and the Ottoman Empire led the Central Powers. Great Britain and France led the Allied Powers. The United States tried to remain out of the war. In 1917, however, events led to a change in policy. In the **Zimmerman Telegram,** Germany asked Mexico to declare war on the United States. In exchange, it offered to help Mexico reclaim U.S. lands it had once controlled. This information helped support those who wanted the U.S. to enter the war. Congress voted to declare war on Germany and the Central Powers in 1917. With U.S. help, the Allies won the war in 1918.

Great Depression

Many factors caused the **Great Depression,** a long economic downturn of the 1930s. The 1920s had a strong economy. People bought many goods on credit, so they had to make payments over time. In time, they stopped buying new goods to pay on their old ones. This reduced the need to make new goods, so some workers lost their jobs. Other people **speculated** on the stock market. This meant they bought stocks to resell when the value went up, which made prices higher than companies were actually worth. The stock market crashed, or lost a huge amount of value, in late 1929. Some investors were ruined. People panicked and took their savings out of banks. Banks ran out of money and had to close.

Voters elected Franklin D. Roosevelt president in 1932. After he took office, Roosevelt began the **New Deal**. The New Deal was a series of federal policies and programs. It offered direct help to people hurt by the Depression. The Civilian Conservation Corps gave people jobs building public works or managing the environment. Unemployment dropped slowly. It was still 14.6 percent in 1940.

The New Deal also made changes to try to stop another Depression from happening. For example, a new federal program insured people's bank deposits. This meant that they could not lose all their savings if a bank failed. The New Deal also began many programs people still use today. For example, one program was Social Security. Social Security makes payments to retired workers.

Key Terms

- alliance
- appeasement
- casualties
- Great Depression
- Holocaust
- New Deal
- nuclear bomb
- speculate
- Zimmerman Telegram

Skills Tip

Reading and analyzing visual information is an important historical skill. Sometimes, you may need to add information from a text to an existing chart or graph. Notice that the text reads *Unemployment dropped slowly. It was still 14.6 percent in 1940.* Suppose you extended the graph by one more year and added this information. What pattern do you see?

U.S. Unemployment Rate, 1929–1940

Source: Journal of Economic Perspectives

President Franklin D. Roosevelt took office in 1933. How did his job programs affect unemployment over time?

World War II

Europe also suffered from the Great Depression. At the same time, it faced problems left from World War I. Strong dictators rose up in Germany and Italy. They helped people feel confident and proud during hard times. But they posed a huge threat to the world. German dictator Adolf Hitler of the Nazi Party threatened his own citizens. He believed certain groups, especially Jews, were inferior. He wanted to wipe them out. During World War II, the Nazis murdered millions of Jewish people in the **Holocaust**.

Hitler gained power in the 1930s. He began to aggressively expand German lands. At first, other European powers let him. They thought he would stop on his own. This policy was called **appeasement**. The policy failed. Germany invaded more and more lands. World War II began in 1939. Germany, Italy, and Japan led the Axis Powers. Great Britain and France led the Allied Powers.

The United States was slow to join the war, but it helped the Allies. On December 7, 1941, Japan attacked the U.S. Navy base at Pearl Harbor, Hawaii. The United States declared war on Japan. Soon, it was also at war with the other Axis Powers. U.S. troops fought in Europe, North Africa, and the Pacific. They helped the Allies triumph over Germany and Italy. Only Japan remained. In 1945, U.S. scientists perfected a powerful new weapon called the **nuclear bomb**. President Harry Truman authorized the use of the bomb against Japan. U.S. forces bombed Hiroshima. Days later, they bombed Nagasaki. Japan surrendered. The war was over.

The nuclear bomb had devastating power. It can flatten buildings across large distances.

Complete the activities below to check your understanding of the lesson content. The Unit 2 Answer Key is on page 152.

Vocabulary

Match each key term with its definition.

1. New Deal
2. appeasement
3. speculate
4. Zimmerman Telegram
5. alliance
6. nuclear bomb

A. German request that Mexico declare War on the United States

B. invest to raise prices and make money

C. policy of letting Hitler take lands

D. federal programs to help people during the Great Depression

E. powerful weapon that could flatten entire cities

F. agreement to work together

Skills Practice

7. Read the paragraph. Then use information from the paragraph to complete the graph by adding the missing bars.

Many U.S. men fought in World War II. U.S. women filled the gap they left in the nation's factories. Women built cars and tanks. They repaired airplanes and made ammunition. In 1940, just 6.7 percent of all iron and steel workers were women. That number rose to 22.3 percent in 1944. Women made up 24.4 percent of all automotive workers in 1944. That was up from just 5.7 percent in 1940. Women always played a big role in the textile industry. Forty-three percent of textile workers were women in 1940. Women increased to 51 percent of all textile workers in 1944.

Women as Percentage of All Workers

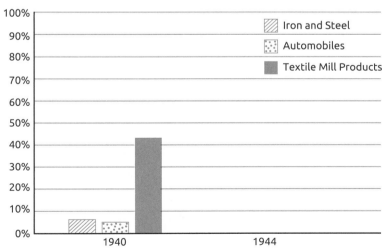

Iron and Steel
Automobiles
Textile Mill Products

REALIZING DEMOCRATIC IDEALS

Key Terms

Civil Rights Movement

Cold War

communism

Equal Rights Amendment

feminism

Jim Crow laws

segregation

sit-in

superpower

Civil Rights Movement

The United States underwent many changes after World War II. It increased equality at home. It also supported democracy abroad.

African Americans had many difficulties after the Civil War. Southern states passed laws that allowed **segregation**. Segregation is the separation of people by race. In the 1890s, the U.S. Supreme Court said segregation was constitutional. It allowed the practice if segregation created "separate but equal" services. But services like education for African Americans were rarely as good as those for white people. **Jim Crow laws** kept them from being able to exercise their rights. The laws unfairly limited voting access. Racism led to violence and terror.

African American leaders worked for civil rights for many decades. Civil rights supporters formed organizations that tried to help African Americans. They tried to persuade the federal government to pass civil rights laws. They also asked for laws banning racial violence, which often went unpunished. But they had little success.

During the 1950s, the **Civil Rights Movement** became more powerful. Leaders protested unfair laws. People held **sit-ins** at segregated businesses. They entered them and refused to leave unless they were served. They boycotted segregated public services like buses. They gathered for peaceful marches. Some white Southerners resisted these efforts. They used violence and fear against civil rights supporters. The movement continued anyway.

Dr. Martin Luther King, Jr. was a well-known civil rights leader. He gave powerful speeches and led protests. He helped convince national leaders to support civil rights. President Lyndon B. Johnson signed key civil rights laws in 1964 and 1965. These ended segregation and expanded voting rights. African Americans still experienced discrimination. But they gained greater legal equality.

Skills Tip

Explicit information is stated directly. Read closely to find explicit details in a text. Explicit details can help you make inferences and draw conclusions that are not stated directly in a text. As you read, practice underlining or highlighting important explicit details. Then, refer to these as you answer questions about a text.

A sit-in protest at an all-white lunch counter in Tennessee, 1960

Rights Movements Expand

The Civil Rights Movement encouraged other groups to call for greater rights. Native Americans organized the American Indian Movement (AIM). They called for the federal government to give Native Americans more control over their lands. Hispanic Americans also worked for greater equality. One important Hispanic leader was Cesar Chavez. He helped organize farm workers in California. They pushed for better wages and working conditions.

The women's rights movement, or **feminism,** spoke loudly during the 1960s and 1970s. Ideas about women's roles changed during this time. Women had always been in the workplace. But middle-class women who worked usually quit when they married and had families. Women also struggled to rise to management jobs. They began to demand equal pay. They wanted laws that ended workplace discrimination. New laws and Supreme Court decisions helped give women more rights at work and in their private lives. Women's groups also wanted a constitutional amendment guaranteeing gender equality. But the **Equal Rights Amendment** was not ratified.

The Cold War

The United States and the Soviet Union had been allies during World War II. This changed after the war ended. Both countries became **superpowers**. A superpower is a country with great political power and influence all around the globe. The United States and Soviet Union had very different views and goals. So, they competed to become the world's only superpower. This competition is called the **Cold War**.

Other countries came to support either the United States or the Soviet Union. Several countries in Western Europe joined the United States in forming the North Atlantic Treaty Organization (NATO). These countries had democratic governments and economies with less government control. The Soviet Union formed an alliance in response to NATO. This was called the Warsaw Pact. It included countries mostly in Eastern Europe. These countries had communist governments. In countries that run under **communism,** the government owns the things used to make and transport products, and there is no privately owned property. They managed the economy closely and had little political freedom.

People worried the superpowers would have a nuclear war. The United States and Soviet Union never fought each other directly in the Cold War. Instead, they gave money and military aid to other countries that were fighting. In the Korean War, the United States supported the democratic forces of South Korea. The Soviet Union helped North Korea. The Korean War lasted from 1950 to 1953. It had no clear winner.

The Vietnam War was fought mostly during the 1960s and early 1970s. The Soviet Union supported the government of North Vietnam. South Vietnam's government was not very democratic, but it opposed the Soviet Union. The United States fought for South Vietnam. They suffered many setbacks. The war became very unpopular in the United States. U.S. forces withdrew, and South Vietnam fell to North Vietnam.

Connect to Today

Europe redrew many borders as the Cold War ended. Strong Soviet-backed governments had united different groups under central governments. When those governments failed, they could not keep the groups together. The former communist country of Yugoslavia is now split into states including Serbia, Montenegro, and Slovenia. Groups there fought a civil war as it split up. Conflict continues in some places. Chechnya is part of Russia, for example, but some Chechens want to be independent. They have fought with others in the region and with Russian troops.

During the 1980s, the Soviet Union began to change. New Soviet leaders tried to help its economy. They reduced government control over some areas. Democratic movements had success in parts of Eastern Europe. Germany, for example, had been split in two after World War II. East Germany had a communist government. West Germany was democratic. In 1990, East Germany ended communist control. It reunited with West Germany. Other states also ended communism. The Soviet Union collapsed in 1991.

During the Cold War, the Berlin Wall was a symbol of the division between the United States and its Western European allies, and the Soviet-controlled East. The wall divided West Berlin and East Berlin from 1961 to 1989.

Complete the activities below to check your understanding of the lesson content. The Unit 2 Answer Key is on page 152.

Vocabulary

Write definitions in your own words for each of the key terms.

1. Cold War _____

_____

2. feminism _____

_____

3. Jim Crow laws _____

_____

4. superpower _____

_____

Skills Practice

Read the excerpt from Dr. Martin Luther King, Jr.'s 1963 "I Have a Dream" speech. Then complete the activities that follow.

And so even though we face the difficulties of today and tomorrow, I still have a dream. It is a dream deeply rooted in the American dream.

I have a dream that one day this nation will rise up and live out the true meaning of its creed: "We hold these truths to be self-evident, that all men are created equal."

I have a dream that one day on the red hills of Georgia, the sons of former slaves and the sons of former slave owners will be able to sit down together at the table of brotherhood.

I have a dream that one day even the state of Mississippi, a state sweltering with the heat of injustice, sweltering with the heat of oppression, will be transformed into an oasis of freedom and justice.

I have a dream that my four little children will one day live in a nation where they will not be judged by the color of their skin but by the content of their character.

5. Where does the speaker say his dream comes from? Underline the details in Paragraph 1 and Paragraph 2 that show the answer.

6. What goal does the speaker have for people in Georgia? Underline this detail in Paragraph 3.

7. What goal does the speaker have for people in Mississippi? Restate his idea in your own words.

_____

_____

8. What goal does the speaker have for the future? Restate his idea in your own words.

_____

_____

Key Terms

Affordable Care Act

foreclosure

Great Recession

guerrilla warfare

Internet

weapons of mass destruction

Connect to Today

You probably use the Internet every day. But this industry did not exist until the 1990s. Do you remember the first time you accessed the Internet? Think about what this suggests about how technology affects change. Inventions and developments can be significant turning points in history.

The United States was the world's only superpower. Technology helped bring the world together. But threats to democracy still existed.

A Technological Boom

The world changed rapidly in the 1980s and 1990s. Cable television brought new voices to the public. Computers had been developed earlier in the 1900s, but they were expensive and cumbersome. New technology allowed computers to become smaller and cheaper. People began to buy home computers. They used them to connect to the **Internet**. People could communicate and share information.

New businesses grew to take advantage of these changes. They made and sold computers. They offered Internet service. Companies began to sell goods over the Internet. Investors put a lot of money into technology companies. Computers also helped companies manufacture goods more cheaply.

Technology allowed people to buy computers like this one for home use. Over time, computers became more powerful and less expensive.

Terrorist Attacks

On September 11, 2001, terrorists attacked the United States. They took control of four airplanes. Attackers crashed two of the airplanes in New York City. They steered the planes into the city's tallest buildings, the Twin Towers of the World Trade Center. The crashes caused great damage. They started fires. Within a short time, the buildings collapsed. About 2,750 people died from the attacks in New York.

At the same time, another plane crashed at the Pentagon, near Washington, DC. The Pentagon is the military's operations center. Researchers believe the terrorists also intended to crash another plane in Washington. But passengers on the plane fought against the terrorists. That plane crashed in rural Pennsylvania.

War in Afghanistan and Iraq War

A terrorist group called al-Qaeda claimed responsibility for the attacks. Americans worried that more would follow. President George W. Bush sent troops to Afghanistan. Analysts believed the leader of al-Qaeda, Osama bin Laden, was hiding there. The Afghan government was unfriendly to the United States. Not long after, Bush also sent U.S. troops to fight in Iraq. He claimed that Iraq was helping terrorists. He also claimed that Iraq had **weapons of mass destruction**. These can be chemical, biological, or radioactive weapons that can damage large areas and kill many people at once. Analysts later determined that Iraq had never had these powerful weapons.

Fighting in Iraq seemed successful at first. Troops quickly toppled Iraq's dictator, Saddam Hussein. But rebuilding a stable nation was extremely difficult. Violence continued around the country. Most Americans had supported the war at first. Over time, public opinion turned. The war did not officially end until 2011.

The war in Afghanistan was also challenging. Afghanistan's government, the Taliban, soon fell. But the new democratic government was not very powerful. Taliban supporters used **guerrilla warfare** against U.S. and allied troops. Guerrilla warfare uses non-traditional tactics, such as ambushes and raids to fight a larger group. Afghanistan remained insecure and dangerous. A U.S. team found and assassinated Osama bin Laden in 2011. But U.S. troops remained in Afghanistan. The war did not end until 2014.

Both wars were very costly. About 4,800 U.S. and allied soldiers died in Iraq. Nearly 3,000 more died in Afghanistan. Tens of thousands of civilians died in Iraq and Afghanistan. The wars also destabilized the region. New extremist groups arose even as democratic movements grew in parts of the Middle East.

> ### Skills Tip
>
> Read carefully to find the sequence of events in a historical text. Remember that texts might talk about events out of order. Pay careful attention to years and sequence words like *soon* and *later* to help you find the correct order.

Economy and Politics

The U.S. economy grew during the early 2000s. Prices for homes soared in parts of the country. This real estate boom fueled building and finance. Changes in banking rules also encouraged investment. But some of these investments were risky at best. Much of the economic growth was based on the hope of more growth. It was not sustainable over time. The economy collapsed in 2007.

The stock market crashed. The federal government agreed to lend billions of dollars to help troubled banks. People lost their homes to **foreclosure**. Foreclosure is the taking back of a property by a lender. Unemployment skyrocketed. Economic troubles spread across the world. The severe downturn was called the **Great Recession**.

In 2008, voters chose Barack Obama as president. He became the first African American to win this office. Obama worked to lessen the problems of the Great Recession. He called for federal investments and policies to help spur economic growth. For example, he called for tax credits for people who bought houses. Obama also helped reform U.S. health insurance. His administration worked with Congress to pass a law called the Patient Protection and **Affordable Care Act**. This law is sometimes called Obamacare. It expanded access to health insurance plans. But it was very controversial. Some people believed the government did not have the power to make these changes. After 2010, Obama lost strong support in Congress.

U.S. Economic Growth, 2005–2014

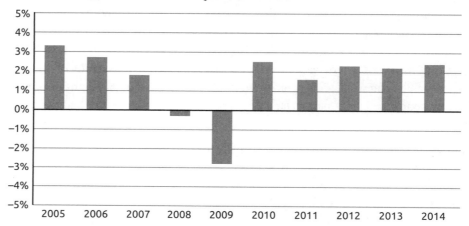

Source: World Bank

A recession happens when the economy shrinks. In what years was the United States in a recession?

Complete the activities below to check your understanding of the lesson content. The Unit 2 Answer Key is on page 152.

Vocabulary

Match each key term with its definition.

1. Great Recession
2. Internet
3. Affordable Care Act
4. foreclosure
5. weapons of mass destruction
6. guerrilla warfare

A. law reforming health insurance
B. severe economic downtown of the 2000s
C. highly destructive materials
D. when a lender takes back property
E. network for communication and exchange
F. non-traditional military tactics

Skills Practice

Read the paragraphs from the lesson. Then choose the correct answer to each question.

Fighting in Iraq seemed successful at first. Troops quickly toppled Iraq's dictator, Saddam Hussein. But rebuilding a stable nation was extremely difficult. Violence continued around the country. Most Americans had supported the war at first. Over time, public opinion turned. The war did not officially end until 2011.

The war in Afghanistan was also challenging. Afghanistan's government, the Taliban, soon fell. But the new democratic government was not very powerful. Taliban supporters used guerrilla warfare against U.S. and allied troops. Guerrilla warfare uses non-traditional tactics. Afghanistan remained insecure and dangerous. A U.S. team found and assassinated Osama bin Laden in 2011. But U.S. troops remained in Afghanistan. The war did not end until 2014.

7. Which event happened first?

    A. Saddam Hussein lost power.
    B. Americans withdrew from Iraq.
    C. Troops assassinated Osama bin Laden.
    D. People found weapons of mass destruction.

8. Which event happened in the same year as the death of Osama bin Laden?

    A. Guerrilla warfare began in Afghanistan.
    B. Public opinion turned against the Iraq War.
    C. The Iraq War ended.
    D. The war in Afghanistan began.

Answer the questions cased on the content covered in this unit. The Unit 2 Answer Key is on page 152.

1. Which factor most supported European colonization of the Americas?

    A. Native civilizations were centered on permanent agricultural settlements.

    B. Europeans transported enslaved Africans over the Middle Passage.

    C. Europeans brought American crops back to Europe.

    D. Native people had no resistance to diseases like smallpox.

Use this excerpt from the Declaration of Independence, written by Thomas Jefferson in 1776, to answer Questions 2–4.

> We hold these truths to be self-evident, that all men are created equal, that they are endowed by their Creator with certain unalienable Rights, that among these are Life, Liberty and the pursuit of Happiness. – That to secure these rights, Governments are instituted among Men, deriving their just powers from the consent of the governed, – That whenever any Form of Government becomes destructive of these ends, it is the Right of the People to alter or to abolish it, and to institute new Government, laying its foundation on such principles and organizing its powers in such form, as to them shall seem most likely to effect their Safety and Happiness.

2. Based on the excerpt, why were the colonists declaring independence?

    A. The British king had not granted them the right of consent of the governed.

    B. Great Britain's government no longer supported their unalienable rights.

    C. Colonists disagreed with the British government about its organizing principles.

    D. The rights of life, liberty, and happiness underlie the formation of governments.

3. Which concept shaped Jefferson's point of view?

    A. natural rights

    B. colonialism

    C. constitutionalism

    D. federalism

4. Which later development best reflects the ideals presented in this excerpt?

    A. organization of the U.S. Congress into two houses

    B. passage of the Northwest Ordinances

    C. ratification of the Articles of Confederation

    D. addition of the Bill of Rights to the U.S. Constitution

5. Manifest destiny is mostly associated with the

    A. outbreak of the American Revolution.

    B. exploration of the Louisiana Territory.

    C. westward expansion of the United States.

    D. granting of voting rights to African Americans.

6. The Civil Rights Movement was most similar to the abolitionist movement in that both

    A. sought to expand liberty and equality to African Americans.

    B. relied mostly on the use of violence to achieve their goals.

    C. were founded during the period of Reconstruction.

    D. failed to win the passage of significant constitutional amendments.

Use this map to answer questions 7–10.

United States, 1861

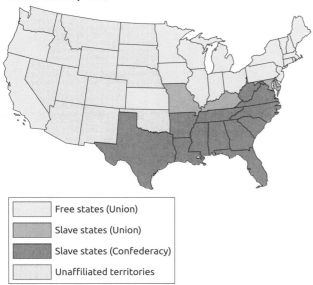

Free states (Union)

Slave states (Union)

Slave states (Confederacy)

Unaffiliated territories

7. This map shows the nation as it was organized during the _____.

8. Based on this map, which of the following is true of unaffiliated territories?

   A. They did not have laws permitting or banning slavery.

   B. They did not experience any battles during the Civil War.

   C. They were not part of the Union or the Confederacy.

   D. They were not subject to federal laws and policies.

9. A historian wants to include this map in an article about Abraham Lincoln's career. Which information should he add to the map?

   A. sites of major Civil War battles

   B. election results from 1860

   C. order in which states rejoined the Union

   D. percentage of African Americans in each state

10. Missouri, Maryland, Delaware, and _____ were the four border states.

11. A historian argues that the Great Depression led to a lasting expansion of the federal government. Which piece of evidence best supports her claim?

    A. New Deal programs like Social Security are still in use.

    B. Unemployment rates nationwide topped 20 percent.

    C. Speculation in the stock market contributed to financial collapse.

    D. Federal job programs built public works and managed resources.

12. Use the information below to complete the graph. Add four bars to the graph to show the unemployment rate in each year.

Many Americans became unemployed during the Great Recession. Unemployment was low before the recession began. Just 4.6% of Americans were unemployed in 2006. But it rose as the economy got worse. By 2008, average unemployment was up to 5.8%. It shot up to 9.3% the following year. Then it grew slightly to 9.6% in 2010 before beginning to go down. Unemployment was barely below 9% in 2011.

U.S. Unemployment Rate, 2008–2011

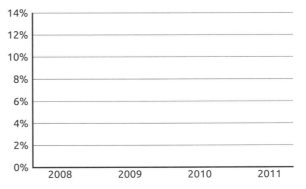

This excerpt is from the "Letter from Birmingham Jail," written by Dr. Martin Luther King, Jr., in 1963.

You deplore the demonstrations taking place in Birmingham. But your statement, I am sorry to say, fails to express a similar concern for the conditions that brought about the demonstrations. I am sure that none of you would want to rest content with the superficial kind of social analysis that deals merely with effects and does not grapple with underlying causes. It is unfortunate that demonstrations are taking place in Birmingham, but it is even more unfortunate that the city's white power structure left the Negro community with no alternative.

In any nonviolent campaign there are four basic steps: collection of the facts to determine whether injustices exist; negotiation; self purification; and direct action. We have gone through all these steps in Birmingham. There can be no gainsaying the fact that racial injustice engulfs this community. Birmingham is probably the most thoroughly segregated city in the United States. Its ugly record of brutality is widely known. Negroes have experienced grossly unjust treatment in the courts. There have been more unsolved bombings of Negro homes and churches in Birmingham than in any other city in the nation. These are the hard, brutal facts of the case. On the basis of these conditions, Negro leaders sought to negotiate with the city fathers. But the latter consistently refused to engage in good faith negotiation. . . .

It is true that the police have exercised a degree of discipline in handling the demonstrators. In this sense they have conducted themselves rather "nonviolently" in public. But for what purpose? To preserve the evil system of segregation. Over the past few years I have consistently preached that nonviolence demands that the means we use must be as pure as the ends we seek. I have tried to make clear that it is wrong to use immoral means to attain moral ends. But now I must affirm that it is just as wrong, or perhaps even more so, to use moral means to preserve immoral ends. . . .

13. This letter is most reflective of the context of

   A. Reconstruction.

   B. the Cold War.

   C. World War II.

   D. the Civil Rights Movement.

14. Based on this excerpt, with which statement would King most likely agree?

   A. The policies of nonviolence are not working.

   B. Segregation is counter to U.S. democratic ideals.

   C. People in Birmingham are all opposed to civil rights.

   D. The Constitution must be amended to abolish slavery.

15. In paragraph 2, King describes the four steps in a nonviolent campaign. The Birmingham demonstrations he writes about fall under which step?

   A. collection of the facts

   B. negotiation

   C. self-purification

   D. direct action

16. To what is King referring when he speaks of "immoral ends" in the last sentence?

   A. holding of demonstrations in Birmingham

   B. actions of the police against protestors

   C. continuation of segregation and racial injustice

   D. imprisonment of civil rights leaders for their actions

Civics and Government

As Americans, we share some ideas that help unite us. Two important ideas are our values and our government institutions. Americans learn about these important aspects of life by studying civics. Civics is the study of the rights and duties of citizens. As an American citizen, you have certain rights as well as responsibilities. For our government to work best, all people—not just a few—must take an active role in governing.

Unit 3 Lesson 1 — ROOTS OF U.S. DEMOCRACY

The United States is a young country. The ideas that helped make American democracy are more than 2,500 years old, however. The founders of the United States built their government on the ideas of **ancient Greece** and Rome. European thinkers from the 1700s and 1800s also shaped American democracy.

What Is Democracy?

Democracy means "rule by the people." In a democracy, citizens rule themselves. This form of government began in the ancient Greek city of Athens. We see two types of democracies: direct democracy and representative democracy. In a **direct democracy**, citizens participate in making all governmental decisions. Athens had a direct democracy. Legal citizens of Athens met to debate and vote in person. Direct democracy is difficult because most countries today are too large and have many citizens.

Key Terms

ancient Greece

ancient Rome

democracy

direct democracy

Enlightenment

natural rights

representative democracy

republic

separation of powers

Connect to Today

Town meetings are a form of direct democracy, giving citizens an opportunity to voice their opinions to help influence decision making. In a democracy, town meetings help remind citizens that the real political power rests with the people. These town meetings have not changed much in more than 200 years.

Vocabulary Tip

The word *democracy* means "rule by the people." It comes from the Greek word *dēmokratiā*. This word is made from the words *dēmos* ("people") and *kratos* ("rule"). You can look for word parts to help you find the meanings of unfamiliar words. Whenever you see a word that ends with *–cracy*, it probably has a meaning about a political system or type of government.

The Roman Republic

As ancient Athens weakened, **ancient Rome** became powerful. The Romans created a new form of government and called it a **republic**. A republic is a form of **representative democracy** in which power rests with citizens. Citizens elect representatives to run the government, make laws, and govern on their behalf. Ancient Rome, the United States, and other modern republics were founded on the idea that true political power rests with the people. Citizens have the right to elect and remove leaders by voting.

The Enlightenment

European thinkers in the 1600s and 1700s challenged the old ways of thinking about science, religion, and government. This movement was known as the **Enlightenment**. Enlightenment thinkers believed that human reason could help better understand the universe and fix social problems. Enlightenment thinkers thought they could gain greater knowledge, freedom, and happiness.

Many Enlightenment ideas influenced the founders of the United States. For example, the ideas of **separation of powers** and **natural rights** became key ideas in American democracy. Separation of powers is the idea that governmental powers should be divided among branches to limit one branch from becoming too powerful. Natural rights are those rights people are born with, such as life, liberty, and the right to own property.

Representative Democracy

The United States is an example of a representative democracy. Most Americans today view a representative democracy, republic, and constitutional republic as the same thing: a government that is limited and in which the people are the true source of power. Citizens elect representatives to make decisions for them. The founders of the United States believed that no government could take away a person's right to life, liberty, and property.

Complete the activities below to check your understanding of the lesson content. The Unit 3 Answer Key is on page 152.

Vocabulary

Match each key word with its definition.

1. natural rights

2. representative democracy

3. the Enlightenment

4. republic

5. ancient Rome

6. direct democracy

7. separation of powers

8. ancient Greece

A. system in which citizens participate in making all governmental decisions

B. the idea that governmental powers should be divided among branches to limit one branch from becoming too powerful

C. a form of democracy in which power rests with citizens

D. civilization that developed the republic form of democracy

E. civilization that developed democracy

F. system in which citizens elect representatives to run the government

G. intellectual movement that challenged ideas about science, religion, and government

H. rights to life, liberty, and property

Skills Practice

Read the excerpts from the primary source documents. Then write complete sentences to answer the questions that follow.

The great and chief end, therefore, of men's uniting into commonwealths, and putting themselves under government, is the preservation of their property. To which in the state of nature there are many things wanting.

First, There wants an established, settled, known law, received and allowed by common consent to be the standard of right and wrong, and the common measure to decide all controversies between them:

—John Locke, from *Two Treatises of Government*, 1691

In order to have this liberty, it is necessary the government be so constituted as one man need not be afraid of another. . . .

When the legislative and executive powers are united in the same body of magistrates, there can be not liberty. . . .

Again, there is no liberty, if the judiciary power be not separated from the legislative and executive. . . .

—Charles de Secondat, Baron de Montesquieu, *The Spirit of the Laws*, 1748

9. Who are the authors of these documents, and which document was written first?

_____

_____

10. According to Locke, what is the key reason people unite into commonwealths, or governments?

_____

_____

11. According to the second passage, what Enlightenment idea does Montesquieu support?

_____

_____

12. In your opinion, what purpose do both Locke and Montesquieu think governments can serve?

_____

_____

_____

FOUNDATIONAL DOCUMENTS

Most countries were formed and united by a common language or heritage. The United States, however, was created out of belief in common values and ideas. These values and ideas are highlighted and explained in two important documents: the **Declaration of Independence** and the **U.S. Constitution**.

Declaring Independence

When the Revolutionary War began in April 1775, most American colonists wanted to protect their rights as British citizens. They did not want to form a separate country. Many colonists changed their minds, however, because of British actions during the first year of the war. Representatives from the states began meeting in May 1776 to push for complete independence from Great Britain.

On July 4, 1776, state representatives announced that they had approved the decision to form a new country. The document that explains this decision is the Declaration of Independence. **Thomas Jefferson** was the chief writer of the Declaration.

Key Terms

amendment

article

Bill of Rights

Declaration of Independence

executive branch

judicial branch

legislative branch

Preamble

Thomas Jefferson

U.S. Constitution

The Declaration of Independence gives many important American democratic ideals. These include the belief that all people are created equal

The Declaration of Independence

The Declaration of Independence contains four main parts. The first part is called the **Preamble**. The Preamble explains why the American colonists created the Declaration of Independence.

The second part is called the Declaration of Natural Rights. This part explains three key ideas. The first idea is that all people are created equal. Each person has the rights to life, liberty, and the pursuit of happiness. The second idea is that the main job of a government is to protect these rights. The third idea is that citizens of a country have the right to form a new government if their rights are taken away.

The third part is called the List of Grievances, or complaints. In this part, the colonists list the complaints they had against the British government. The grievances include imposing taxes without consent, cutting off trade with other parts of the world, waging war against the colonies, and housing British soldiers in the colonies.

The fourth and final part is called the Resolution of Independence. In this part, the colonists declare their independence from Great Britain. This independence gives the states the right to act in matters of war, trade, and agreements with other countries. It is important to note that the Declaration of Independence did not officially give the colonists their independence. Only victory in the Revolutionary War would do that.

The Constitution of the United States of America

The Constitution of the United States of America is the oldest written constitution among the major countries in the world. The Constitution is the highest authority of law in the United States. It also creates the rules for how the national government operates. Other parts of the Constitution describe the rights and freedoms of American citizens.

Connect to Today

Each year, Americans celebrate on the Fourth of July. It is a national holiday. Americans go to picnics and watch parades and fireworks. The day celebrates the passage of the Declaration of Independence on July 4, 1776. The Declaration is a symbol of the United States of America. It represents our system of government and our most important values, such as equality, liberty, and freedom.

What Is in the U.S. Constitution?

The Constitution is made up of three main parts. The first part is called the Preamble. The second part contains seven sections called **articles**. Each article describes and defines a certain part of the government. The third part contains the **Bill of Rights** and additional changes to the Constitution, called **amendments**.

The Preamble is the introduction. In this short passage, the writers clearly state that the power of the U.S. government comes from the people. The rest of the Preamble outlines six key purposes of the government.

The second part of the Constitution is divided into seven articles, each identified by a Roman numeral. Articles I, II, and III describe the powers and responsibilities of the three branches of the national government: the legislative, executive, and judicial branches.

Skills Tip

The writers of the Constitution used Roman numerals to organize content within the document. Use this basic chart to help you understand Roman numerals when reading about the U.S. Constitution.

1 = I	6 = VI
2 = II	7 = VII
3 = III	8 = VIII
4 = IV	9 = IX
5 = V	10 = X

Article I	Outlines the powers and responsibilities of the **legislative branch**—Congress. • Congress's main responsibility is to make laws for the country. • Congress is divided into two chambers, the Senate and the House of Representatives.
Article II	Creates and describes the **executive branch**, which includes the president. • The executive branch makes sure that the nation's laws are carried out.
Article III	Establishes the **judicial branch**. • The judicial branch makes sure laws are interpreted fairly. • The judicial branch is also in charge of hearing cases in courts of law.

Articles IV–VII describe how the national government and the states work together. These articles also talk about the relationships between the national government and the states.

The final part of the Constitution contains the changes, or amendments, made to the Constitution. The first 10 amendments are known as the Bill of Rights. The U.S. Constitution has been amended 27 times in the country's history.

Complete the activities below to check your understanding of the lesson content. The Unit 3 Answer Key is on page 152.

Vocabulary

Write definitions in your own words for each of the key terms.

1. Preamble _____

_____

2. articles _____

_____

3. legislative branch _____

_____

4. Thomas Jefferson _____

_____

Skills Practice

Read the excerpts from the primary source documents. Then write complete sentences to answer the questions that follow.

> "We hold these truths to be self-evident, that all men are created equal, that they are endowed by their Creator with certain unalienable Rights, that among these are Life, Liberty and the pursuit of Happiness.--That to secure these rights, Governments are instituted among Men, deriving their just powers from the consent of the governed. . . ."
>
> —from the Declaration of Independence

5. According to the Declaration, how does government get its power?

_____

_____

> "We the People of the United States, in Order to form a more perfect Union, establish Justice, insure domestic Tranquility, provide for the common defence, promote the general Welfare, and secure the Blessings of Liberty to ourselves and our Posterity, do ordain and establish this Constitution for the United States of America."
>
> —from the Constitution of the United States

6. How does this passage from the Constitution support the ideas in the Declaration of Independence?

_____

_____

_____

The Bill of Rights contains the first 10 amendments to the U.S. Constitution. These amendments guarantee certain rights to all American citizens. The Bill of Rights also places limits on how the government can use its power over Americans.

The First Amendment

One of the main purposes of the Bill of Rights is to protect Americans' **civil liberties**. Civil liberties are those rights that the government is required to protect. These rights include the freedoms we have to think, speak, and act without the government interfering and without the fear of unfair treatment.

The First Amendment protects five rights, or freedoms. These are the freedom of religion, freedom of speech, freedom of the press, freedom of assembly, and freedom to petition the government.

Freedom of speech and freedom of the press allow Americans and the media to voice their opinions. They can do so without fear of punishment. Freedom of religion protects citizens' rights to freely practice their religions. The freedom to assemble and the right to petition the government give Americans the power to gather peacefully. They can also bring their concerns to the government.

Key Terms

bail

civil liberties

civil case

due process

federal

searches and seizures

violated

Connect to Today

The First Amendment keeps Congress from restricting the freedom of the press. When the Bill of Rights was written, newspapers and printed materials were the only media available. These were created on printing presses. Today the "the press" includes all media, including radio, television, and Internet sources.

During colonial times, Americans spread political ideas on pamphlets printed on presses like this one. How do people spread political ideas today?

Americans can use these freedoms as long as they do not limit the rights and freedoms of others. Americans do not have the right to use their freedoms in ways that might lead to violence or public disruption.

The Second and Third Amendments

The Second Amendment protects the rights of Americans to own firearms. The Third Amendment says that soldiers cannot be housed in a citizen's home during peacetime without the owner's permission. Soldiers can be housed in citizens' homes during wartime with the proper legal authority. These amendments are designed to help protect citizens from the government.

Amendments that Guarantee Fair Legal Treatment

Several amendments in the Bill of Rights establish our rights to fair legal treatment. The Fourth Amendment protects citizens from "unreasonable **searches and seizures**." This means the government cannot search or take an American's home or property without a very good reason.

The Fifth Amendment protects the rights of those accused of crimes. This amendment requires the government to follow proper constitutional procedures in trials and in other actions it takes against individuals. This is often called the right to **due process**.

The Sixth and Eighth Amendments also protect the rights of people accused of crimes. The Sixth requires the government to explain and describe the exact charges against the accused. This amendment also states that those accused are allowed a speedy and fair trial by jury. Also, an accused individual is entitled to have a lawyer. The Eighth Amendment prevents the government from charging high **bail** amounts. The Eighth also protects the accused from cruel and unusual punishment.

The Seventh Amendment describes and protects the rights of people who are involved in **civil cases**. These are lawsuits that involve disagreements, rather than crimes, between people. Individuals in these cases are also guaranteed the right of a trial by jury.

The Ninth Amendment

The Ninth Amendment prevents the government from claiming that the only rights citizens have are those listed in the Bill of Rights. The amendment implies that Americans have other rights. These rights are not described in the Constitution. It guarantees that these other rights cannot be taken away.

The Tenth Amendment

The Tenth Amendment protects the states and citizens from the **federal** government. The federal government is also called the national government. This amendment states that the Constitution gives the federal government certain powers. Powers not given to the federal government are held by the states and the people. The amendment supports the idea that the federal government can only use powers given to it in the Constitution. This stops Congress and the president from becoming too strong.

Connect to Today

The U.S. government created the Patriot Act after the terrorist attacks on September 11, 2001. This law became a new tool to fight terrorism. Members of Congress and some citizens thought parts of the act **violated** the Fourth Amendment. They believed the government was violating rights against unreasonable searches and seizures. Americans learned in 2013 that the government was also collecting information on some American citizens' phone calls and Internet usage. Are there times when the government should be allowed to violate our Fourth Amendment rights?

Complete the activities below to check your understanding of the lesson content. The Unit 3 Answer Key is on page 153.

Vocabulary

Complete each sentence with a key term from the lesson.

1. _____ means that the law or government cannot treat individuals unfairly or unreasonably and must follow constitutional rules.

2. The national government is also called the _____ government.

3. The Fourth Amendment protects Americans from unreasonable _____, in which the government might take a citizen's property without a good reason.

4. The freedoms of speech, religion, petitioning the government, and assembling peacefully are called _____.

Skills Practice

Read the paragraph about free speech written by Benjamin Franklin. Then write complete sentences to answer the questions that follow.

"Freedom of speech is a principal pillar of a free government; when this support is taken away, the constitution of a free society is dissolved, and tyranny is erected on its ruins. Republics and limited monarchies derive their strength and vigor from a popular examination into the action of the magistrates."

5. Why does Franklin think free speech is important?

_____

_____

6. In your opinion, would Franklin have been a strong supporter of the Bill of Rights?

_____

_____

_____

THREE BRANCHES OF GOVERNMENT

The Constitution describes how the national government is organized. The government is divided into three branches: legislative, executive, and judicial. Each branch has its own powers and responsibilities. Dividing the government into three branches prevents any one of the branches from becoming too powerful. This is called **separation of powers**.

Legislative Branch

The legislative branch is made up of the House of Representatives and the Senate. Together they are known as **Congress**. Both the House and the Senate meet in separate chambers inside the U.S. Capitol in Washington, DC. Each Congress is given a number to identify it. The Congress elected in 2016 will be the 115th since Congress first met in 1789.

Both houses of Congress meet in the U.S. Capitol. The Senate chambers are located in the north wing. The House of Representatives meets in a large chamber in the south wing.

Congress is the national **legislature**—a government body that makes the nation's laws and decides how the government's money is spent. The two chambers of Congress are separate but have an equal role in the creation of laws. Congress also has the power to declare war and **regulate**, or control, interstate and foreign commerce.

The House of Representatives

The House of Representatives is the larger body of Congress. It has 435 members. Each member represents a congressional district in his or her home state. States with larger populations are given more representatives in the House. Representatives hold their offices for two years.

Key Terms

ambassador

Cabinet

Congress

diplomat

foreign policy

judicial review

legislature

regulate

separation of powers

terms

verdict

Skills Tip

You can figure out the meaning of an unfamiliar word by using context clues from the sentence or paragraph. If you don't know what *chambers* means, look at the ideas and other words in the sentence that you do understand. You can see that the sentence is describing meetings. It also contains the phrase "inside the U.S. Capitol." That phrase is a clue to the meaning of *chambers*.

THREE BRANCHES OF GOVERNMENT

The Senate

The Senate has 100 members, or senators. Each state elects two senators to represent its citizens. Senators hold their offices for six years. Unlike members of the House, who represent the citizens in their districts, senators represent all the citizens of their states.

In both the House and the Senate, the political party to which more than half of the members belong is known as the majority party. The other party is called the minority party. Majority party members are selected to be in charge of the various committees in the House and Senate. This gives the majority party greater power and influence.

The Executive Branch

The executive branch includes the President and Vice President. This branch also includes many offices, departments, and workers. The main responsibility of the executive branch is to make sure that laws passed by Congress are carried out.

The president is the leader of the executive branch. The president serves a term of four years and can only serve two **terms**. Presidents are chosen in presidential elections by the votes of Americans in all 50 states.

The President's Roles

The president is the chief of state and represents all Americans. The president meets with foreign leaders and travels around the world representing the United States. The president is also the nation's chief **diplomat**. In this role, the president directs the nation's **foreign policy** by choosing **ambassadors** and making treaties with other countries.

The president is also the commander in chief of the United States military. In this role, the president can give orders to the military and direct operations. Congress has the authority to monitor and sometimes change the president's actions.

Helping the President

Fifteen departments help the president run the executive branch. Each department manages a different area of government. For example, the Department of the Treasury runs the nation's finances. The Department of State carries out foreign policy. The department leaders all serve as members of the president's **Cabinet**. The Cabinet helps the president make decisions and develop policies.

The Judicial Branch

The judicial branch is made up of different federal courts that review and evaluate laws. These courts also interpret the Constitution. The main job of the judicial branch is to make sure that the nation's laws are justly enforced and that everyone in the United States receives equal justice under the law. The federal court system is made up of three kinds of courts.

District and Appellate Courts

District courts are the lowest level in the federal court system. These courts hear civil and criminal cases that involve federal issues or constitutional rights. Almost all federal cases begin in district courts. There are 94 district courts in the United States with at least one in every state.

Appellate courts are also called appeals courts. These courts hear cases that were originally decided in district courts. People who lose their cases in a district court can ask an appeals court to review the decision. An appeals court can either uphold or overturn the original **verdict,** or ruling, or it can order another trial.

The Supreme Court

The U.S. Supreme Court is the highest court in the federal court system. Its main job is to decide whether laws are allowable under the U.S. Constitution. Almost all the cases that the Supreme Court hears are those that have been appealed from lower district courts.

The Court is made up of a chief justice and eight associate justices. Justices are chosen by the president but must be approved by the Senate. Supreme Court justices are appointed to the position for life.

The Power of the Supreme Court

The Supreme Court is the final court to which anyone can appeal a legal decision in the United States. All lower courts must follow decisions made by the Supreme Court. Even the executive and legislative branches of government must obey its decisions.

The Supreme Court gets much of its power and influence from the idea of **judicial review**. This means that the Court can review any federal, state, or local law to see if it is allowed by the Constitution. Judicial review makes the Supreme Court the highest authority to interpret the meaning of the Constitution.

Vocabulary Tip

Connect key terms that are related to each other. The word *judicial* comes from the Latin language and means "of or belonging to a court of justice." Noticing words that are related to judiciary, such as judge and justice, can you help define and remember unfamiliar words.

Complete the activities below to check your understanding of the lesson content. The Unit 3 Answer Key is on page 153.

Vocabulary

Complete each sentence with one of the key terms. Each term is used exactly once.

foreign policy	separation of powers	Cabinet	judicial review	Congress

1. _____ allows the Supreme Court to review federal, state, and local laws to make sure they are constitutional.

2. Developing relationships with other countries and protecting U.S. interests around the world is called _____.

3. The concept of _____ divides the federal government into three branches to prevent any one branch of becoming too powerful.

4. The group of department leaders who advise the president is called the _____.

5. The House of Representatives and the Senate combined make up _____.

Apply Your Knowledge

Label each responsibility as a duty of the legislative, executive, or judicial branch.

6. develop foreign policy _____

7. write the nation's laws _____

8. decide whether federal laws are constitutional _____

9. serve as commander in chief _____

10. control the nation's taxing and spending _____

11. consider court cases that involve constitutional rights _____

Read the following passage and study the political cartoon. Then answer the questions that follow.

In 1974 the Supreme Court decided the case *United States* v. *Nixon*. The case involved audio recordings that President Richard Nixon had made in his White House office. Congress was investigating Nixon's role in illegal activities that members of his administration had committed. Investigators believed the tapes would provide important evidence. Nixon refused to hand over the tapes to Congress. The Supreme Court ruled in favor of Congress and forced Nixon to release the tapes.

Opper Project, The Ohio State University Cartoon Research Library

12. What does the cartoon suggest about the relationship between Nixon's executive branch and the legislative branch?

_____

_____

13. In what way does *United States* v. *Nixon* illustrate separation of powers?

_____

_____

_____

BALANCING POWER

Key Terms

agenda

bills

checks and balances

concurrent powers

enumerated powers

federalism

framers

impeach

popular sovereignty

reserved powers

supremacy clause

veto

Skills Tip

Main ideas are the most important ideas in a paragraph, section, or chapter. Supporting details are facts or examples that explain the main idea. Locating the main idea and its supporting details is an essential skill when reading texts about social studies. This skill will help you remember key information about the content. Often, a section heading or the first sentence of a paragraph can help you figure out the main idea.

You learned in a previous lesson that the **framers**, or creators, of the Constitution constructed a government with three branches. This was one way they hoped to keep any one branch from becoming too powerful. The Constitution also contains other measures to help balance the powers of government.

Balancing Power Between the Federal and State Governments

One of the main ideas in the Constitution is **popular sovereignty**. This means "authority of the people." Citizens agree to be governed, but the government must follow certain rules. The opening words of the Constitution, "We the People," support this idea. Many Americans worried that a strong national government would lead to the loss of basic rights and misuse of power. The framers created a limited government and restricted its authority to certain powers granted by the people.

The framers realized that a strong federal government was necessary. But they also knew that the citizens and the states should have some authority as well. The Constitution takes some, but not all, powers away from the states. This system of shared power is called **federalism**. The U.S. federal system allows citizens of each state to handle their needs in their own way. The system also allows states to work together to deal with issues that affect the entire country.

Three Kinds of Power

The Constitution describes three kinds of government powers. Some powers are held by only the federal government. These are called **enumerated powers**. These powers are described clearly in the Constitution. The power to create money, regulate interstate and foreign trade, maintain the armed forces, and manage federal courts are examples of enumerated powers.

Powers that stay with the states are called **reserved powers**. These include the power to establish schools, set up local governments, and regulate trade within the state. The Constitution does not specifically list these powers. However, the 10th Amendment states that all powers not granted to the federal government are "reserved to the States."

The third kind of powers defined by the Constitution are called **concurrent powers**. These powers are shared by the federal and state governments. Concurrent powers include the right to collect taxes, borrow money, provide for public welfare, and set up courts and prisons. Article VI of the Constitution contains the "**supremacy clause**." This recognizes the Constitution and federal laws as supreme when in conflict with those of the states.

Balancing Power within the Federal Government

You have learned about the three branches of government. This system is one way power is shared and balanced within the federal government. The Constitution also creates a system of **checks and balances** to prevent any one of the three branches from becoming too powerful. Within this system, each branch has ways to check, or limit, the power of the other branches.

As head of the executive branch, the president has broad powers. The president can propose bills, appoint judges, and **veto**, or reject, acts of Congress. Many executive branch powers can be checked by the other branches. For example, the Senate has the power to approve or reject the president's nominations and treaties. Congress has the power to **impeach**, or formally accuse officials from the other branches of wrongdoing.

The Supreme Court can declare laws passed by Congress unconstitutional. It can do the same with executive actions taken by the president. The powers of the judiciary branch are balanced by the other two branches. The president can nominate judges or judicial branch officials, but the Senate must confirm or reject these nominations. Once a judge is approved by the Senate, he or she can hold the job for life. This is one way that federal judges maintain independence from the other branches.

Balancing Powers When Creating Laws

Lawmaking provides an example of how powers are shared and balanced in the government. Only members of Congress have the power to introduce **bills** for consideration. However, the executive branch often suggests legislation it would like passed. This is because every president has a legislative **agenda**, or plan. These are new laws that the president wants Congress to pass.

To become a law, a bill must be passed in an identical form by both houses of Congress. Once this happens, the bill is sent to the president. The president can check the power of Congress by vetoing the bill. If the president vetoes the bill, the bill is sent back to Congress. Congress, however, can overturn the president's veto. If two-thirds of both houses vote to support the bill, the bill becomes a law.

Connect to Today

The Line Item Veto Act became law in 1997. This law gave presidents the power to veto certain parts, or lines, of spending bills passed by Congress. Supporters of the act thought that the line item veto would prevent wasteful spending. Before then, all bills had to be either signed or rejected in whole. In 1998, the Supreme Court ruled that this act was unconstitutional. The Court stated that the act gave too much power to the president because it violated the power of Congress to control all spending as described in Article I of the Constitution.

Complete the activities below to check your understanding of the lesson content. The Unit 3 Answer Key is on page 153.

Vocabulary

Write definitions in your own words for each of the key terms.

1. federalism _____
   _____

2. concurrent powers _____
   _____

3. impeach _____
   _____

4. bills _____
   _____

5. agenda _____
   _____

6. veto _____
   _____

Choose the correct answer to each question.

7. What is the desired effect of checks and balances?

   A. The president must get Congress's approval for all executive actions.

   B. The Congress must create a balanced budget.

   C. The judicial branch controls the government.

   D. No one branch of government becomes too powerful.

8. Popular sovereignty means

   A. the most popular bills become law.

   B. authority of the people.

   C. rule by the government.

   D. the most populated states have the most power.

9. Enumerated powers are those that are

   A. given only to Congress and clearly described in the Constitution.

   B. reserved by the state governments.

   C. shared by the executive and legislative branches.

   D. additional powers granted to Congress by the Supreme Court.

Skills Practice

Read the excerpt from Article I, Section 7 of the U.S. Constitution. Then complete the activities that follow.

> Every Order, Resolution, or Vote to which the Concurrence of the Senate and House of Representatives may be necessary (except on a question of Adjournment) shall be presented to the President of the United States; and before the Same shall take Effect, shall be approved by him, or being disapproved by him, shall be repassed by two-thirds of the Senate and House of Representatives, according to the Rules and Limitations prescribed in the Case of a Bill.

10. In what way is the process described in Article I, Section 7 an example of checks and balances?

    _____

    _____

    _____

11. In your opinion, why did the framers of the Constitution decide that each chamber of Congress and the president must be made aware of all bills and issues debated in Congress?

    _____

    _____

    _____

Key Terms

extradition

full faith and credit

infrastructure

republican

territories

Skills Tip

A fact is something that can be proven or documented. It does not change unless new evidence disproves it. An opinion expresses the viewpoints or feelings of a person. Opinions can change from person to person, but facts are true. Learning how to distinguish fact from opinion will help you to critically evaluate and question what you read.

Most Americans have more contact with their state and local governments than with the federal government. This means that your state government has a great influence on your daily life and activities.

State Governments

As you have learned, the Tenth Amendment to the Constitution states that all powers not given to the federal government are held by the states. This means that state governments are necessary to meet the needs of their citizens. The federal government requires that each state have a **republican** form of government. In this government system, citizens elect representatives to run the government. Each of the 50 states also has its own constitution. All provisions of state constitutions must comply with the U.S. Constitution.

Most state governments follow the federal government in how they are organized. All states have a governor who serves as the head of the executive branch in his or her state. All states, except Nebraska, have two houses in their legislative branch. Each state has its own court system. These court systems differ in how they are structured.

Each state has its own National Guard commanded by the governor of the state. National Guard troops are a part of the armed forces and work with local governments and the federal government during natural disasters or other emergencies.

The Roles of State Governments

The U.S. Constitution forces state governments and the federal government to work together on some issues. Criminal investigations and national defense are two examples. States also must cooperate with the other states. This is called **"full faith and credit"** clause. For example, legal decisions and marriage and driver's licenses issued in one state must be honored in other states. States must also follow **extradition** rules. Extradition is when a state sends a person accused of a crime back to the state in which the supposed crime was committed.

An important job of state governments is to monitor and regulate local governments in the state. Local governments get authority from the state government. A state government has the power to break up a local government or combine it with other governments. Another key job of state government is to manage the education system in the state.

Most states have a department or board of health. These departments operate health education and disease prevention programs. This helps provide for public health and safety. States are also responsible for issuing many types of licenses and for managing elections.

States are also responsible for building and maintaining much of their own **infrastructure**. That is the basic equipment and structures, such as roads, water lines, and bridges, that are needed for an area to function properly. Most of the states have departments of highways and public works to do this work. These departments oversee the construction of roads, bridges, and important public buildings.

Connect to Today

The American flag has a star for each state. Left off the flag are stars for the five U.S. **territories** in which American citizens live. These territories are Puerto Rico, Guam, the Northern Marianas, United States Virgin Islands, and American Samoa. Citizens in the territories have local voting rights and protections under U.S. federal courts. Elected officials represent the territories in the U.S. House of Representatives. They have the same powers as other members but cannot cast official House of Representative votes.

Complete the activities below to check your understanding of the lesson content. The Unit 3 Answer Key is on page 153.

Vocabulary

Complete each sentence with a key term from the lesson.

1. Highways, bridges, and public buildings are all part of a state's _____.

2. States must respect legal decisions and licenses from other states because of the _____ clause in the U.S. Constitution.

3. A system of government in which citizens elect officials to run the government is called a _____ government.

Apply Your Knowledge

Label each power as a responsibility belonging either to state governments or to the federal government.

4. develop foreign policy _____

5. establish schools and an educational system _____

6. make money _____

7. issue driver's licenses _____

8. declare war on foreign countries _____

9. maintain roads and bridges within a state _____

MUNICIPAL GOVERNMENTS

Local governments affect the daily lives of most Americans. Local government representatives live and work near the people they represent. This makes local governments more responsive to the needs and concerns of their citizens.

Municipal Governments

Municipal governments govern cities and towns. Most towns and cities have a mayor. A mayor serves as the city's chief executive. The legislative branch of local governments is made up of a group of elected representatives. This group is often called the city council. These officials have the power to enact new local laws and regulations called **ordinances**.

A key role of a city government is to provide for the daily needs of its citizens. Maintaining police and fire departments and public works services are important city responsibilities. Public works include streets and the city's sewer systems. Other city departments run public libraries and parks. City workers also issue building permits and regulate zoning laws.

Special District Governments

A **special district** is a unit of government that has a key purpose. Education, water supply, and transportation are examples. **School boards** are special districts. A school board makes many of the decisions that affect the public school systems. This includes buying textbooks, hiring school workers, and managing school construction projects.

Other Local Governments

Counties are the largest local government unit. County governments often provide services for citizens who do not live in cities or towns. Counties provide law enforcement and health services and take care of roads. County officials also keep official records.

Townships are one of the smallest units of local government. A township is a land and political subdivision within a county. Most townships are run by a group of officials known as a township committee, board of supervisors, or board of trustees.

Key Terms

municipal

ordinance

school board

special district

township

Complete the activities below to check your understanding of the lesson content. The Unit 3 Answer Key is on page 153.

Vocabulary

Match each key term with its definition.

1. ordinances
2. townships
3. school boards
4. special districts
5. municipal

A. land and political subdivision within counties

B. group of elected officials that manages an educational system

C. having to do with governing a city or town

D. local government laws or regulations

E. a government unit within a larger municipal government

Apply Your Knowledge

Label each statement as a description of municipal, county, special district, or township governments.

6. often provides services for people who do not live in cities or towns _____

7. has a specific role to perform within a larger government _____

8. usually led by an official whose title is mayor _____

9. sometimes governed by a group called the board of trustees _____

All Americans play a part in making our communities safe and successful. Being active in the political process also helps keep our towns alive and strong. How else do Americans show strong citizenship qualities?

Basic Rights of Americans

As American citizens, we enjoy certain basic rights. One right is security. We expect the government to protect us if necessary. Security also means that we expect to be protected *from* the government. The government cannot take away our Constitutional rights. Another basic right is equality. All Americans expect to be treated equally under the law. **Liberty**, or freedom, is another basic right.

Civic Duties

American **citizenship** brings with it certain civic duties and responsibilities. Duties are actions that are required by law. Responsibilities are voluntary actions. Through these actions, we help make sure that our government can protect everyone's rights and meet our needs. The U.S. government does require its citizens to perform the following duties: obey laws, pay taxes, defend the nation if needed, serve on juries, and attend school.

Rights and Responsibilities

Civic responsibilities are not required by law. But they are just as important as civic duties. An important responsibility is being informed. American citizens should know what their government is doing. This is helpful when expressing opinions or getting ready to vote. Another important responsibility is voting. By voting, citizens can help shape the future of their towns and their governments.

Americans are also expected to respect the rights and property of other Americans. Accepting the rights of others to have different opinions and live different lives is called **tolerance**. All citizens are also expected to contribute to the **common good**. This means they work to promote the health and **welfare**, or well-being, of everyone.

Key Terms

citizenship

common good

liberty

naturalization

tolerance

welfare

Naturalization Process

The process required to become a citizen is called **naturalization**. To become a U.S. citizen, noncitizens must meet several legal requirements. First, they must sign a document stating a desire to become an American citizen. Then, they must meet with an official of the U.S. Citizenship and Immigration Services. They must also pass an English language and American civics test. The final step is to take the Oath of Allegiance. This is a promise to be loyal to the United States.

The Oath of Allegiance requires people to make several other promises. They must give up loyalty to other countries. They promise to defend the Constitution and laws of the United States. They also promise to serve in the U.S. military if needed and to perform important work for the nation when necessary. After taking the Oath of Allegiance, they are U.S. citizens.

New citizens take the Oath of Allegiance as part of a naturalization ceremony.

Connect to Today

In a democracy, citizens must be willing to take part in civic life. The Internet has changed the way Americans take part in democracy. It has made it easier for citizens to stay informed and to participate meaningfully in our democracy. Today, local, state, and federal governments have their own websites. These websites make it easy for citizens to learn about new laws or programs. Citizens can request services and participate directly in government.

Complete the activities below to check your understanding of the lesson content. The Unit 3 Answer Key is on page 153.

Vocabulary

Write definitions in your own words for each of the key terms.

1. naturalization _____

   _____

2. common good _____

   _____

3. tolerance _____

   _____

4. responsibilities _____

   _____

5. duties _____

   _____

Skills Practice

Read the quote from President John F. Kennedy. Then complete the activities that follow.

In your hands, my fellow citizens, more than mine, will rest the final success or failure of our course. Since this country was founded, each generation of Americans has been summoned to give testimony to its national loyalty. The graves of young Americans who answered the call to service surround the globe. . . .

And so, my fellow Americans: ask not what your country can do for you—ask what you can do for your country.

6. Circle words or phrases from the passage that relate to the duties and responsibilities of American citizens.

7. Based on the passage, what do you think President Kennedy's opinion is on the role of common Americans in a democracy?

   _____

   _____

   _____

Key Terms

black codes

discrimination

Seneca Falls Convention

suffrage

women's rights movement

It took many years and the hard work of citizens before the Bill of Rights covered all Americans equally. More amendments to the Constitution extended the rights of Americans.

Women's Rights Movement

In the 1800s, American women did not have full legal rights. In the mid-1800s, some women began demanding greater rights. In 1848, Lucretia Mott and Elizabeth Cady Stanton organized the **Seneca Falls Convention**. This gathering in Seneca Falls, New York, was the beginning of an organized **women's rights movement**.

Stanton and others wanted the movement to work toward the goal of gaining women the right to vote. The right to vote is also called **suffrage**. By 1918, many states, but not all, had granted women the right to vote. Several women's rights groups pressured Congress to pass a constitutional amendment. In August 1920, after three-fourths of the states had ratified it, the Nineteenth Amendment, guaranteeing women the right to vote, went into effect.

Civil Rights Movement

Three amendments were added to the U.S. Constitution soon after the Civil War. These amendments extended basic rights to African Americans. The Thirteenth Amendment made slavery illegal and freed African Americans. The Fourteenth Amendment defined a United States citizen as anyone "born or naturalized in the United States." This made most African Americans full citizens. The Fifteenth Amendment says that no state may take away a person's voting rights because of race.

As you learned in Unit 2, African Americans still experienced segregation and **discrimination**, or unfair treatment. Some states passed laws called "**black codes**" that kept African Americans from being hired for jobs other than farming and being a servant without applying for a license. These laws also limited their property rights and restricted them in other ways.

Efforts for African American civil rights date back to the 1800s. Founded in the early 1900s, organizations like the National Association for the Advancement of Colored People (NAACP) and the National Urban League worked to help get more opportunities for African Americans. Organizations like the National Association for the Advancement of Colored People (NAACP) and the National Urban League worked to help get more opportunities for African Americans.

Many people supported the Civil Rights Movement. The movement became stronger in the 1950s and 1960s. Rev. Martin Luther King, Jr., and others organized peaceful marches and protests. In 1964 and 1965, President Lyndon Johnson signed civil rights laws. These laws expanded voting rights and ended segregation.

Other Amendments that Expanded Rights

Several other new amendments have expanded the rights of Americans. It was not until 1961 that citizens of Washington, DC, could vote in national elections. The Twenty-third Amendment secured this right for them.

Originally, the Constitution did not state a minimum age for voters. Over the years, most states set the minimum at 21. Many younger Americans thought that this was unfair. American teens had fought in the military in all of the nation's wars yet could not vote. The Twenty-sixth Amendment guaranteed the right to vote to citizens 18 and older for all national and state elections.

Skills Tip

Author's purpose is the reason an author has written a text. Authors write to inform readers about factual information or to describe a sequence. Authors might also write to entertain readers with humor or with a story. Authors can write to persuade readers. Ask yourself the following questions to determine an author's purpose for writing: Did the author give me information (to inform)? Did the author give an opinion (to persuade or convince)? Did the author make me laugh (to entertain)?

Complete the activities below to check your understanding of the lesson content. The Unit 3 Answer Key is on page 153.

Vocabulary

Complete each sentence with a key term from the lesson.

1. The start of an organized women's movement was at the _____.

2. Even with the addition of the Thirteenth, Fourteenth, and Fifteenth amendments, African Americans still faced _____.

3. A main goal of the _____ was the right of women to vote.

4. Some states passed _____ that restricted the rights of African Americans.

5. The right to vote is also called _____.

Skills Practice

Read the excerpt from the Fourteenth Amendment. Then write complete sentences to answer the questions that follow.

Amendment XIV

Section 1.

All persons born or naturalized in the United States, and subject to the jurisdiction thereof, are citizens of the United States and of the state wherein they reside. No state shall make or enforce any law which shall abridge the privileges or immunities of citizens of the United States; nor shall any state deprive any person of life, liberty, or property, without due process of law; nor deny to any person within its jurisdiction the equal protection of the laws.

6. On what level of government does this section of the amendment focus?

    _____

    _____

7. Why do you think many Americans thought it necessary to pass the Fourteenth Amendment?

    _____

    _____

The right to vote is one of the major responsibilities of U.S. citizens. Doing so gives people the power to influence government and the laws that govern them. Elections give voters the chance to select leaders and hold them accountable for their performance in office.

The U.S. Election Process

The U.S. political system has four general types of elections. These are primary and general elections, issue elections, and special elections. Electing **candidates** to political office is a two-part process. The first part is the **nomination** of candidates in a primary election. Primary elections narrow the field of candidates. Voters then choose candidates for various offices in a general election.

In some elections at the state or local level, voters may vote on issues as well as candidates. The **initiative**, for example, is a way that citizens can propose new local laws or state laws. The **referendum** is a way for citizens to approve or reject a state or local law.

Some state and local governments can have special elections. A **runoff election** is held when none of the candidates for an office wins a majority of the vote in the general election. The runoff is held to determine the winner. The recall is another type of special election. Some states allow citizens to vote to remove a public official from office. Voters may recall an official because they do not like his or her position on issues or because the official has been charged with wrongdoing.

Key Terms

candidate

convention

Electoral College

Federal Election Commission

hard money

initiative

nomination

political parties

referendum

runoff election

soft money

Presidential Elections

In all elections except presidential elections, the candidate who gets a majority of the popular vote is elected to office. In the presidential election, voters actually vote for a group of electors. These electors then place the votes that decide who becomes president. The electors are part of the **Electoral College**. Each state gets an electoral vote for each member it has in Congress. The total number of electoral votes is 538. The candidate who receives a majority of votes in the Electoral College wins the election.

Role of Political Parties

The Constitution does not discuss **political parties**. However, the first political parties formed only a few years after the country was created. A political party is a group of individuals that organizes to win elections, run the government, and set policy. Today, the United States has several political parties. Two parties, the Democrats and the Republicans, are the most powerful.

POLITICAL PARTIES, CAMPAIGNS, AND ELECTIONS

Skills Tip

When you read, you make connections between what you are reading and what you already know. The more connections you make, the better you are able to understand. You may make connections between the text and a personal experience. You can also connect the text to another text or to historical or current events that you heard about in the news.

Delegates from each state attend presidential nominating conventions. These delegates help choose the party's nominee.

The main job of political parties is to nominate candidates to run for public office. The major parties are organized at the local, state, and national levels. Each party also has a national committee made of representatives from every state. This committee helps raise money for elections and organizes the party's national **convention**. A convention is a large gathering every four years before the presidential election. At the convention, the party nominates its candidates for president and vice president. Party officials also write the party platform at the convention. A platform is a document that outlines the party's position on a variety of issues.

Political parties also play a role in helping citizens take part in government. Citizens can use their parties to communicate with government leaders. This ensures that government officials represent the interests of the people.

Paying for Election Campaigns

Candidates and political parties spend a great amount of time and effort raising money for elections. Approximately $7 billion was spent during the 2012 presidential election. Congress and the Supreme Court have established the ways money can be raised for elections. The **Federal Election Commission** (FEC) is the government agency that monitors all federal election laws and campaign spending.

Vocabulary Tip

The word *party* has several meanings. It can describe a social gathering. It can also describe a group of people that has gathered for a special purpose. You have also read that *party* is the word for an organized political group. Words that are spelled and pronounced the same way but have different meanings are called homonyms.

Hard money is the term used to describe money given by individuals or groups directly to candidates. The amount of hard money people and groups can give is limited. Candidates must also release information about who gives money and how that money is spent.

Presidential elections are also funded by public money. Citizens can choose to donate $3 when they fill out their income taxes. The major candidates can then split this money. However, they must agree not to take any other direct donations.

Most campaign money comes from private sources. A major source of money comes from Political Action Committees (PACs). PACs are organizations that support favored candidates. Laws passed by Congress allow political parties to raise soft money. **Soft money** includes donations that are used for general purposes and do not go to a specific candidate. Limits on soft money donations are not as strict.

Complete the activities below to check your understanding of the lesson content. The Unit 3 Answer Key is on page 153.

Vocabulary

Complete each sentence with a key term from the lesson.

1. The _____ is the government agency in charge of federal elections.

2. The _____ is made up of 538 delegates from all the states.

3. Money given by individuals directly to a candidate is called _____.

4. Every four years, the major political parties gather for a _____.

Skills Practice

Read the excerpt from James Madison on political parties, or factions. Then write complete sentences to answer the questions that follow.

> All civilized societies would be divided into different sects, factions, and interests, ... of rich and poor, debtors and creditors, ... the inhabitants of this district or that district, the followers of this political leader or that political leader, the disciples of this religious sect or that religious sect. . . . In all cases where a majority are united by a common interest or passion, the rights of the minority are in danger.

5. Based on Madison's statement, what opinion do you think he has about political parties?

   _____

   _____

6. What evidence in the excerpt supports your answer to question 5?

   _____

   _____

7. According to Madison, what harm would political parties cause?

   _____

   _____

LANDMARK SUPREME COURT DECISIONS

Amendments to the Constitution guaranteed rights to Americans. But African Americans and other groups still did not enjoy civil rights. Some Americans looked to the U.S. Supreme Court to secure their rights.

Dred Scott v. Sandford (1857)

The Supreme Court's decision in *Dred Scott* v. *Sandford* is one of its most controversial. This case was decided during a time when the country was in deep conflict over slavery. Dred Scott was a slave whose slaveholder moved him to the free state of Illinois and to the territory that is now Minnesota. Scott claimed that since he now lived in free areas, he should be free. Scott sued his slaveholder, John Sandford. The Supreme Court ruled that a slave was property and not a citizen. This meant that slaves had no rights under the Constitution. This decision created more tension between the North and the South.

Plessey v. Ferguson (1896)

Louisiana passed a law that required trains to have "equal but separate" cars for white and African American riders. The *Plessey* v. *Ferguson* case challenged that law. The Court ruled that the **equal protection clause** of the Fourteenth Amendment allowed "separate but equal" cars. The equal protection clause is a part of the Fourteenth Amendment requiring states to guarantee the same rights and protections to all citizens. *Plessy* v. *Ferguson* **upheld**, or agreed with, the "separate but equal" idea that states would use later to pass segregation laws.

Brown v. Board of Education (1954)

The Supreme Court **overturned**, or reversed, the *Plessey* v. *Ferguson* decision in *Brown* v. *Board of Education*. It also abolished the "separate but equal" doctrine. The justices ruled that schools separated by race are unequal simply because they are separate. The Court stated that segregation violated the equal protection clause of the Fourteenth Amendment. The decision in this case goes beyond public education. It covers almost all public places and activities.

Gideon v. Wainwright (1963)

Clarence Earl Gideon was accused of committing a felony. Because he was very poor, he asked the judge to provide him with an attorney free of charge. The judge denied his request. Gideon then asked the Supreme Court to hear his case. The Court ruled for Gideon, saying that the Sixth Amendment requires poor criminal defendants to be provided an attorney free of charge. The opinion stated that the right to a lawyer is a fundamental right essential to a fair trial.

Miranda v. Arizona (1966)

The case of *Miranda* v. *Arizona* considered the rights people have while in police custody. Ernesto Miranda confessed to rape and kidnapping after hours of police questioning. He was found guilty but appealed the decision because of his confession. The Supreme Court later ruled that police must inform suspects of their rights before questioning. Today, these rights are known as the **Miranda Warning**.

The typical Miranda Warning states: "You have the right to remain silent. Anything you say or do can and will be held against you in a court of law. You have the right to speak to an attorney. If you cannot afford an attorney, one will be appointed for you. Do you understand these rights as they have been read to you?"

Connect to Today

Individuals and groups have looked to protect their civil rights since the nation's founding. Many of these people have relied on the Supreme Court to guarantee their rights. In 2015, the Court ruled in *Obergefell* v. *Hodges* that state bans on same-sex marriage are unconstitutional. The decision guaranteed the right of same-sex couples to get married.

Roe v. Wade (1973)

The Supreme Court's decision in *Roe* v. *Wade* is one of its most debated. At the time of the decision, most states restricted or banned abortions. *Roe* v. *Wade* challenged these laws. The Supreme Court ruled that women have the right under the Constitution to decide whether to terminate a pregnancy. The Court stated that individuals have a constitutional right to privacy and that abortion was part of a woman's zone of privacy. The ruling legalized a woman's right to an abortion under certain circumstances.

Complete the activities below to check your understanding of the lesson content. The Unit 3 Answer Key is on page 153.

Vocabulary

Write definitions in your own words for each of the key terms.

1. overturned _____

    _____

2. equal protection clause _____

    _____

3. upheld _____

    _____

4. Miranda Warning _____

    _____

Match the descriptions below with the correct landmark Supreme Court case.

Roe v. Wade	Brown v. Board of Education	Miranda v. Arizona
Plessey v. Ferguson	Gideon v. Wainwright	Dred Scott v. Sandford

5. required police to tell a suspect his rights while in custody _____

6. overturned the "separate but equal" doctrine _____

7. established the "separate but equal" doctrine _____

8. established the right of women to terminate a pregnancy in certain situations _____

9. guarantees the right to have an attorney during a trial _____

10. early civil rights case that ruled that African Americans were not citizens _____

Some challenges our country faces have been around for a long time. Some issues are new. Rapid social, political, and technological changes are forcing us to address some of the most important issues in our nation's history.

Immigration

Immigration has always been controversial in this country. Many people who are against it argue that immigrants take jobs and social services away from Americans. Immigration supporters point out that immigrants contribute to the U.S. economy. They argue that immigrants often take jobs no one else wants.

Much of the immigration debate concerns illegal immigrants, also called **undocumented immigrants**. Large numbers of immigrants from Mexico and Central America have come illegally. Most come to the United States to find better jobs and more opportunities. Many, however, end up working in low-paying jobs, such as migrant farmwork, and receive no benefits.

Congress has tried to limit illegal immigration by punishing employers who hire illegal immigrants. Congress also gives resident status to those who have lived in the United States for a certain number of years. This is called **amnesty**. Those who oppose amnesty argue that immigrants should not be rewarded with legal status for breaking immigration laws.

The term "**DREAMer**" has been used to describe young, undocumented immigrants who were brought to the United States as children. These people have lived and gone to school in the United States. Many DREAMers consider themselves Americans. The DREAM Act is a proposed bill that would provide a pathway to U.S. citizenship for some DREAMers. A few versions of the DREAM Act have been introduced in Congress, but none have passed. The act would require DREAMers to either join the military or go to college.

Relative Power of the Federal Government

One of the key ideas in the U.S. Constitution is that of a limited national government. The framers feared that a strong national government would misuse power. The Constitution describes and limits the power of the federal government. The Bill of Rights and the amendments also limit the powers of the government.

President Franklin D. Roosevelt used the government to help people get through the Great Depression. This increased the size of government greatly. Several presidents who followed also believed that government should play a large role in American society. The government has continued to have major influence in the economy and in providing social programs.

Many Americans today think that our federal government is too big and powerful. They argue that it creates more problems than it solves. They also argue that government social programs have become too costly and that too many rules keep businesses from growing.

U.S. government agencies have been secretly collecting information about emails and phone calls. This is part of the war against terrorism. Supporters of these activities argue that they are necessary to protect the country. Others say that these actions violate constitutional rights.

Key Terms

amnesty

bias

Citizens United v. Federal Election Commission

dark money

DREAMer

Federal Election Campaign Act

Affordable Care Act

undocumented immigrant

Skills Tip

When reading about a controversial issue, it is important to analyze the point of view of the texts you read. A point of view is the position from which something or someone is observed. Most people have a point of view, or **bias**, which influences the way they interpret issues. Recognizing bias will help you judge the accuracy of what you read. Ask yourself questions like these: What is the purpose of the text? Which statements are facts or opinions? What evidence of bias is present?

Opponents of the decisions in the *Citizens United* case protest in New York City. Why might people disagree about the effects of this decision?

Campaign Finance Reform

Campaign finance reform has been debated for decades. Congress passed the **Federal Election Campaign Act** (FECA) in the 1970s. This act and its amendments limited how campaigns raised money. Many Americans were worried that too much money was being spent on elections. They believed wealthy people and groups were influencing candidates with large money donations.

Congress passed another law to limit money in elections. In 2010, this law was challenged. The Court overturned the law with its ruling in *Citizens United v. Federal Election Commission*. The Court ruled that corporations and labor unions could spend unlimited amounts of money on political ads and other tools. **Dark money**, or secret political donations, given to nonprofit groups, has increased greatly. These groups do not have to report who gives the money.

Health Care

Health care has also become a controversial issue. President Barack Obama changed the country's health care system during his first term. In 2010, Congress passed the **Affordable Care Act**, nicknamed "Obamacare." The act required all Americans to buy health insurance. The federal government and the states provided money to help poorer Americans pay for it.

Supporters of the act argued that the new law would make getting health insurance much easier and less expensive. They also thought that parts of the law would prevent unfair insurance practices and slow the rising costs of health care. Most important, they argued, was that tens of millions of uninsured Americans would get health care coverage.

All Republicans in Congress voted against the act. In 2012 and again in 2015, the Supreme Court upheld most parts of the Affordable Care Act. However, the act remained controversial. Critics of the act argue that it will increase health insurance prices for some Americans who were already insured.

Critics also argued that it would lead to government control of the health care industry. Critics say this was another example of the federal government becoming too big and powerful. Many also argued that forcing Americans to buy health care insurance was unconstitutional.

Complete the activities below to check your understanding of the lesson content. The Unit 3 Answer Key is on page 154.

Vocabulary

Complete each sentence with a key term from the lesson.

1. The _____ is a law passed in 2010 that requires all Americans to have health insurance.

2. _____ are young, undocumented immigrants who have grown up in the United States.

3. The term _____ is used to describe secret money donated to nonprofit groups.

4. A writer's point of view, or _____, influences the way he or she interprets and writes about issues.

Skills Practice

Choose the correct answer to each question.

5. What was the effect of *Citizens United* v. *Federal Election Commission?*

   A. Campaign money was strictly limited.

   B. Dark money given to nonprofit groups increased.

   C. All campaign donations had to be reported to the FEC.

   D. Donations from wealthy individuals dropped greatly.

6. Giving amnesty to an illegal immigrant means

   A. the immigrant is given the means to return to his or her home country.

   B. the immigrant is immediately given full U.S. citizenship.

   C. the immigrant is permanently denied entry into the United States.

   D. the immigrant is given legal status, and prior illegal immigration actions are dismissed.

7. The 2010 act known as Obamacare dramatically changed the nation's

    A. social services system.

    B. campaign finance system.

    C. health care system.

    D. immigration system.

8. A result of the Federal Election Campaign Act was

    A. campaigns were free to collect as much money as possible.

    B. campaigns were limited in how they could raise money.

    C. campaigns were required to use only government-provided money.

    D. campaigns were no longer allowed to take donations from individuals.

Skills Practice

Read the excerpt from the President Ronald Reagan. Then complete the activities that follow.

"In this present crisis, government is not the solution to our problem; government is the problem. From time to time, we have been tempted to believe that society has become too complex to be managed by self-rule, that government by an elite group is superior to government for, by, and of the people. But if no one among us is capable of governing himself, then who among us has the capacity to govern someone else? All of us together, in and out of government, must bear the burden."

—Ronald Reagan, First Inauguration, 1981

9. Based on this excerpt, what do you think Reagan's point of view of government is?

_____

_____

10. In your opinion, would Reagan favor a large, powerful federal government or a smaller, limited federal government?

_____

_____

Answer the questions based on the content covered in this unit. The Unit 3 Answer Key is on page 154.

1. Which of the following best describes why the United States is a representative democracy?

   A. Every citizen gets to vote on key issues.

   B. Each state has the exact number of representatives in Congress.

   C. Citizens elect representatives to make decisions for them.

   D. Each citizen is entitled to at least one representative.

2. Which level of government is usually responsible for maintaining your local parks and school playgrounds?

   A. federal government

   B. state government

   C. township government

   D. municipal government

Read the following passage to answer questions 3 and 4.

This statement is from the administration of President Barack Obama.

The DREAM Act is common-sense legislation drafted by both Republicans and Democrats that would give students who grew up in the United States a chance to contribute to our country's well-being by serving in the U.S. armed forces or pursuing a higher education. It's good for our economy, our security, and our nation. That's why the DREAM Act has long enjoyed bipartisan support. It's limited, targeted legislation that will allow only the best and brightest young people to earn their legal status after a rigorous and lengthy process, and applies to those brought to the United States as minors through no fault of their own by their parents, and who know no other home.

3. Based on the statement, why does the Obama administration argue that Congress should pass the DREAM Act?

   A. It would be good for our economy, our security, and our nation.

   B. The act would make it tougher for immigrants to go to college.

   C. The act is popular with both Democrats and Republicans.

   D. Young immigrants would be able to stay in their homes.

4. Which statement best explains the purpose of this White House statement?

   A. The statement is trying to convince Republicans to support the DREAM Act.

   B. The statement is trying to persuade people to support the DREAM Act.

   C. The statement is trying to convince immigrants to support the DREAM Act.

   D. The statement is trying to explain how easy legal immigration can be.

5. Which document describes the American colonists' decision to form their own government?

   A. the Pledge of Allegiance

   B. the Bill of Rights

   C. the Declaration of Independence

   D. the U.S. Constitution

6. *Match each power to the correct government branch box in the table.*

write the nation's laws	decide whether federal laws are constitutional
serve as commander in chief	control the nation's taxing and spending
consider constitutional rights cases	develop foreign policy
ensure laws are justly enforced	impeach government officials
appoint ambassadors	

Legislative	Executive	Judicial

7. What is the main difference between a civic duty and a civic responsibility?

   A. Duties help the country, but responsibilities only help individuals.

   B. Duties are required by law, and responsibilities are voluntary.

   C. Government officials perform duties, and common citizens perform responsibilities.

   D. Responsibilities are required by law, and duties are voluntary.

8. Which of the following did the writers of the Constitution provide in their framework of government to make sure that no branch of government could become too powerful?

   A. three separate branches of government, each with different powers and responsibilities

   B. a Supreme Court with the power of Judicial Review

   C. a Congress made up of two houses

   D. presidential veto power

9. Which amendment in the Bill of Rights protects the freedom of speech and the freedom of the press?

   A. Sixth Amendment

   B. Second Amendment

   C. Fourth Amendment

   D. First Amendment

Read the following quotes from former Congresswoman Shirley Chisholm to answer questions 10–12.

"That I am a national figure because I was the first person in 192 years to be at once a congressman, black, and a woman proves, I would think, that our society is not yet either just or free."

—from *Unbought and Unbossed*

"Discrimination against women, solely on the basis of their sex, is so widespread that it seems to many persons normal, natural, and right. . . . The argument that this amendment will not solve the problem of sex discrimination is not relevant. . . . Of course laws will not eliminate prejudice from the hearts of human beings. But that is no reason to allow prejudice to continue to be enshrined in our laws—to perpetuate injustice through inaction.

The time is clearly now to put this House on record for the fullest expression of that equality of opportunity which our founding fathers professed. . . .

They professed it, but they did not assure it to their daughters, as they tried to do for their sons. . . .

The Constitution they wrote was designed to protect the rights of white, male citizens. As there were no black Founding Fathers, there were no founding mothers—a great pity, on both counts. It is not too late to complete the work they left undone. Today, here, we should start to do so."

—speech in the House of Representatives, August 10, 1970

10. Based on information in both quotes, what is unique about Shirley Chisolm's point of view?

    A. She is a mother and a member of Congress.

    B. She has personally experienced discrimination.

    C. She is a woman and an African American.

    D. She was the first woman elected to Congress.

11. What is Chisolm's view of equality as constructed by the framers of the Constitution?

    A. Equality was rightly granted to and protected for all Americans.

    B. Not granting women equal rights was the proper decision at the time.

    C. Equality as constructed by the framers should not be changed.

    D. Only protecting equal rights for white, male citizens was wrong and shortsighted.

12. What course of action does Chisolm recommend?

    A. She recommends that Congress should begin to grant full equality to women.

    B. Chisolm suggests that Congress should not reverse the work of the founding fathers.

    C. Chisolm recommends establishing laws outlawing all forms of prejudice.

    D. Chisolm recommends rewriting the Constitution.

13. Progress in gaining civil rights for many Americans has come because of

    A. Supreme Court decisions.

    B. states granting more and more rights to their citizens.

    C. citizen-supported state referendums.

    D. constitutional amendments added in the 1900s.

14. The two stages of elections in the federal election process are

    A. general and recount elections.

    B. general and recall elections.

    C. primary and general elections.

    D. primary and special elections.

Economics

We hear the word *economy* all the time. Reporters and politicians say things like, "The economy is improving," or "It looks like the economy might be facing some trouble." What are these people talking about? What makes the economy strong or weak? This unit will look at what the economy is and how it functions.

Real GDP Growth

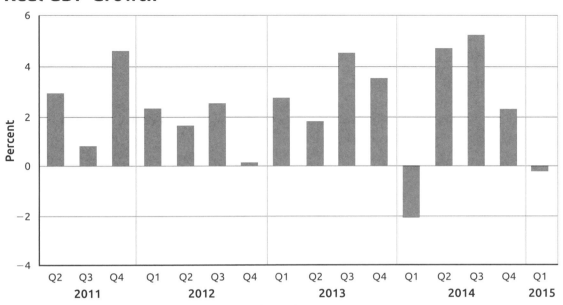

Real GDP growth is measured at seasonally adjusted annual rates.

Source: U.S. Bureau of Economic Analysis

Since 2011, the size of the U.S. economy has grown nearly every quarter. This means the economy has generally been getting stronger. It got weaker at the beginning of 2015.

Unit 4 Lesson 1   BASIC ECONOMIC QUESTIONS

What Is the Economy?

The economy is all around us. Anywhere that people are making things, buying and selling things, or using things—the economy is there. Economists have special terms for these activities. Making things is called **production**. Production requires **resources**, which are supplies of things. Buying and selling things is called **voluntary exchange.** Exchanges take place between producers and consumers. Using things is called **consumption**.

BASIC ECONOMIC QUESTIONS

Key Terms

allocate

consumer

consumption

exchange

free-market system

goods

opportunity cost

producer

production

profits

resources

scarcity

services

utility

voluntary exchange

Producers are the people who make things. They **allocate**, or divide and give out, resources to produce and distribute goods. **Consumers** purchase and use these **goods and services**. In general terms, economics is about the allocation of resources for the production and distribution of goods and services that people consume.

Making Economic Decisions

Economic activity involves a lot of decisions. To understand economics, it's important to realize that people value goods and services differently. Economists use the term **utility** to describe how useful a person finds a particular good or service. That's how much they value it. Utility is very personal. Some people like apples more than others do. Some people value free time more than money, while others would rather have more money than more free time.

So how do people make economic decisions? According to economists, they try to maximize their utility. They **exchange**, or trade, goods and services to get the most that they can. To maximize utility, you have to consider **opportunity cost**. Opportunity cost is what you give up when you make a decision.

Suppose that you decide to exercise every day between 9 am and 11 am. It's clear what you get from this decision: greater fitness. What you give up (the opportunity cost) is everything else you could do with those two hours. If you could have studied French during that time, you'd be giving up learning how to speak French. If you choose to exercise during that time, an economist would say that you value fitness more than the ability to speak French.

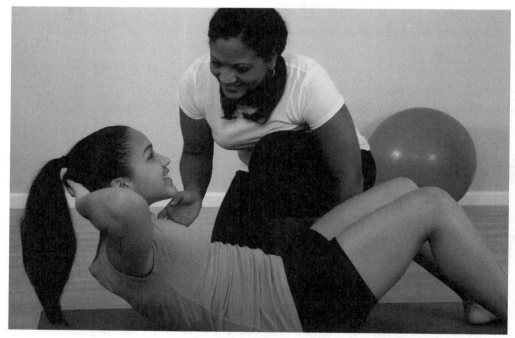

Choosing to exercise is an economic decision. The opportunity cost of that decision is the benefit you might have gotten if you had chosen to do something else.

124

Scarcity and the Three Basic Questions

Humans have wants and needs that are often greater than what's available. It's a sad fact of life, but it's true. People face **scarcity** every day.

We saw before that economics is about the allocation of resources for the production and distribution of goods and services that people consume. The problem of scarcity is the reason this is necessary. If there were plenty of goods and services to go around, we wouldn't need to make allocation decisions.

Because scarcity is a fact of life, people work to increase the availability of what they want and need. If there were unlimited resources, everyone could have everything they want. But we don't have unlimited resources. We often have to make tough decisions about what to do with the resources that we do have.

This brings up the three basic questions of economics. These are the questions that every society answers to organize its economy:

- What is to be produced?
- How is production organized?
- For whom are goods and services produced?

In a **free-market system,** these questions are answered by producers. For producers in a free-market system, utility is measured by **profits**. Producers try to maximize profits, or the money made after costs and expenses are paid. Here's how producers answer the three basic questions of economics:

- **What is to be produced?** Something that consumers value and will purchase.
- **How is production organized?** As efficiently as possible.
- **For whom are goods and services produced?** Everyone and anyone who will buy them.

Skills Tip

You can figure out the meaning of an unfamiliar word by using context clues from the sentence or paragraph. If you don't know what *scarcity* means, look at the ideas in the first paragraph that you do understand. You can see "*wants and needs that are often greater than what's available.*" That phrase is a clue to the meaning of *scarcity*.

In a free-market system, production is organized through the free choices of producers. Producers try to make profits by producing what consumers want the most.

Complete the activities below to check your understanding of the lesson content. The Unit 4 Answer Key is on page 154.

Vocabulary

Write definitions in your own words for each of the key terms.

1. allocate _____

   _____

2. scarcity _____

   _____

3. opportunity cost _____

   _____

4. free-market system _____

   _____

Choose the correct answer to each question.

5. Which term describes the sale of a car?

   A. allocate

   B. goods

   C. exchange

   D. utility

6. Which term is used to describe a decision made by a producer?

   A. allocate

   B. consumption

   C. profits

   D. resources

Skills Practice

Match each situation with the basic economic question it answers.

7. A computer company decides to sell its least expensive laptops to elementary schools throughout the nation.

8. A chef opens a restaurant that specializes in pizza and pasta.

9. A car factory uses an assembly line to give each worker a specific task to perform.

A. What is to be produced?

B. How is production organized?

C. For whom are goods and services produced?

Prices

Prices affect everything in the economy. The price of housing affects where you will live. The price of labor affects how much you get paid for your work. And the prices of goods and services determine how much of something you can buy. The way prices are set, and how they change, is at the heart of economics.

The Law of Supply and Demand

Prices in a free-market system are set by the Law of Supply and Demand. **Supply** is the amount of a good or service that is produced. **Demand** is the amount of that good or service that consumers want.

Economists have a special way of talking about supply and demand. They refer to quantity supplied and quantity demanded. **Quantity supplied** is the amount of something that producers are willing to sell at a certain price. The higher the price, the more producers are willing to sell. **Quantity demanded** is the amount of something that consumers are willing to buy at a certain price. The lower the price, the more consumers are willing to buy.

Take a slice of pizza, for example. At $0.00, producers are willing to sell exactly zero slices of pizza, since they would lose money. Therefore, the quantity supplied at $0.00 is zero. But as the price increases, the supply will increase as well. At a price of $5.00, producers will be falling all over themselves to make pizza because they'll earn a big profit on each slice.

The quantity demanded for $0.50 slices of pizza is very high because almost everybody would be willing to buy at that price. The quantity demanded for $4.50 slices of pizza is low since few people would be willing to pay that price.

The price for any good or service is where the quantity supplied and the quantity demanded are the same. This is known as the **market equilibrium**.

Price	Quantity Demand	Quantity Supplied
$5.00	0	1,000
$4.50	100	900
$4.00	200	800
$3.50	300	700
$3.00	400	600
$2.50	500	500
$2.00	600	400
$1.50	700	300
$1.00	800	200
$0.50	900	100
$0.00	1,000	0

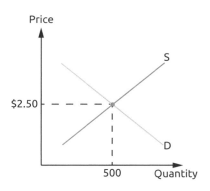

The table to the left shows the quantity demanded (D) and quantity supplied (S) for a slice of pizza. The graph above shows that the Law of Supply and Demand produces a price of $2.50. At this price the demand for pizza equals the supply, and 500 slices of pizza will be sold.

INTRODUCTION TO SUPPLY AND DEMAND

Changes in Supply and Demand

The economy is almost never standing still. Changes occur all the time. Prices rise and fall. But why? The answer is simple: changes in either supply or demand or both. A change in supply or demand creates a **shortage** or a **surplus**, pushing prices up or down in predictable ways.

The rules for how changes in supply and demand affect prices are simple.

Change	Curve	Effect	Reason for Price Change
Supply goes up	Supply curve shifts to the right	Price goes down	This creates a surplus, so consumers have more choices. This makes compete more to meet the demand. They must lower prices to lure consumers.
Supply goes down	Supply curve shifts to the left	Price goes up	This creates a shortage, so consumers have to compete for the goods they want. They have to be willing to pay more to win this competition.
Demand goes up	Demand curve shifts to the right	Price goes up	This leads to a shortage, so consumers are competing more. They have to be willing to pay more to win this competition.
Demand goes down	Supply curve shifts to the left	Price goes down	This creates a surplus because there's more supply than consumers want. Producers need to compete with each other. This pushes them to drop prices.

Supply and demand can change for all kinds of reasons. One is a **supply shock.** This occurs when there's a sudden shortage of some good. For example, suppose that a hurricane sinks a large number of fishing boats. The supply of fish would drop suddenly. That would shift the supply curve to the left, changing the market equilibrium. The price would go up and the quantity would go down as shown in the graph to the left.

Demand can easily change too. Suppose that a famous actor begins wearing white pants all the time. This creates a trend. More consumers demand white pants. This pushes the demand curve to the right. The new market equilibrium would be a higher price and a higher quantity produced.

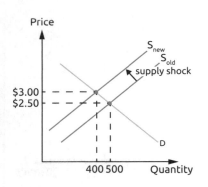

Suppose that there's a sudden shortage in flour available for pizza dough. This graph shows how this supply shock shifts the supply curve to the left, raising the price of a slice of pizza and lowering the quantity produced.

Complete the activities below to check your understanding of the lesson content. The Unit 4 Answer Key is on page 154.

Skills Practice

Write "up" or "down" to complete the sentences below.

1. Two new companies begin making cell phones. Cell phone prices will go _____.

2. Most people stop wearing hats. Hat prices will go _____.

3. One of a town's two restaurants closes. Prices at the remaining restaurant go _____.

4. More people begin riding bicycles. Gasoline prices will go _____.

5. Every state requires bicycle-riders to wear helmets. The price of bicycle helmets will go _____.

Use the following graphs to answer questions 6–8 below.

A.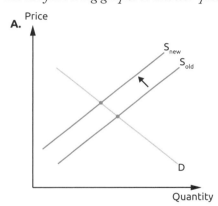

B.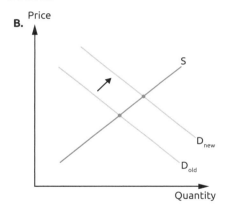

C.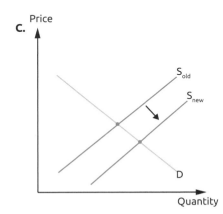

D.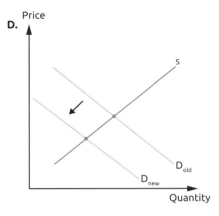

6. Which graph shows a situation where the market equilibrium price goes up because of a supply shock? _____

7. Which graph shows the reason why gasoline prices rise in the summer? _____

8. Which graph shows the result of a new trend? _____

SUPPLY AND DEMAND IN ACTION

Key Terms

average

buying power

cost-push inflation

demand-pull inflation

derived demand

inflation

labor

labor market

labor pool

median

wages

The Labor Market

In the economy, every good and service is subject to the Law of Supply and Demand. That includes **labor**, which is a special service that is used to make goods and services. Just as there are markets for cars and pizza and cell phones, there's also a market for labor. In the **labor market**, the prices paid for the service provided is called **wages**.

A Special Market

The labor market differs from other markets in certain ways. In most markets, demand comes from consumers. In the labor market, demand comes from producers. That makes the demand for labor a **derived demand**. A car factory only needs workers if there's a demand for the cars it makes. So the car factory's demand for workers is derived from consumers' demand for cars.

We saw before that changes in either supply or demand shift the supply or demand curve, changing the market equilibrium. The same kind of thing happens in the labor market. In the labor market, these shifts in the supply or demand curve take place for particular reasons.

Suppose that gas prices go up. This tends to reduce consumer demand for large vehicles such as SUVs and pickup trucks that have lower gas mileage than smaller vehicles. This change not only affects the market for SUVs and pickup trucks, it impacts the labor market as well. It reduces the demand for workers in SUV and pickup truck factories.

Other factors such as population growth, education, and immigration also affect labor markets. A boom in the population during one decade will increase the size of the **labor pool** about two decades later. The labor pool is the source of trained people from which workers can be hired. If more people go to college, the labor pool for jobs that require a college education will go up a few years later. When immigration goes up, so does the size of the labor pool.

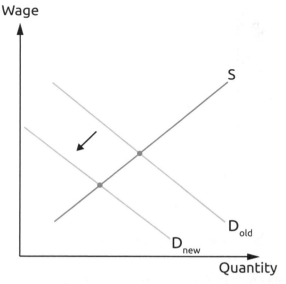

This graph shows how a rise in gas prices affects the labor market for workers in SUV and pickup truck factories. Reduced demand for these kinds of vehicles lowers wages for workers who make them.

Inflation

The graph below shows a steady rise in average wages and median household income between 1990 and 2013. This doesn't mean that workers got richer during that period. That's because there was also a steady **inflation** in prices during the same period. Inflation makes the **buying power** of a single dollar go down. Something that cost $5.00 in 1990 would've been $8.91 in 2013.

Inflation might seem like a bad thing, but it's a constant presence in the economy. As time passes, things always get more expensive. As long as inflation is accompanied by rising wages, then the rise in prices doesn't matter very much because consumers will have more money to spend.

The normal process of inflation results from changes in supply and demand. One source of rising prices is **demand-pull inflation**, which is a rise in prices driven by rising consumer demand. When an economy is growing, consumers often demand goods faster than they can be supplied. This shifts the demand curve to the right, leading to a rise in prices. In this case, consumers "pull" prices upward because of their increasing demand.

There's a second, related cause of inflation. As prices go up because of demand-pull inflation, workers need more money to buy the same amount of goods as before. This puts an upward pressure on wages. It also leads to an increase in other production costs. Demand-pull inflation means that companies must pay more for the resources that go into production. With rising costs of labor and other production costs, companies have to raise prices to cover their higher costs. This is called **cost-push inflation**.

U.S. Income, 1990–2013

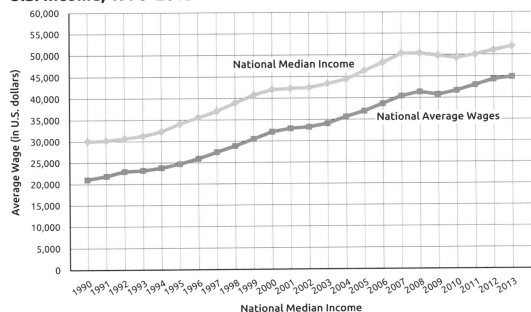

Sources: U.S. Census Bureau and U.S. Social Security Administration

The average wage increased by 113% between 1990 and 2013 while the median household income went up by 73%. During the same period, the price of a $5.00 good increased by 78% to $8.91.

Complete the activities below to check your understanding of the lesson content. The Unit 4 Answer Key is on page 154.

Skills Practice

Choose the correct answer to each question.

1. Which of these occurs when the population of a country grows quickly?

    A. Buying power increases.

    B. Cost-push inflation speeds up.

    C. Demand-pull inflation slows down.

    D. The labor supply curve shifts to the right.

2. A rise in demand for cell phones would lead to which change in the labor market in the cell phone industry?

    A. The supply curve would shift to the right, raising wages.

    B. The supply curve would shift to the left, lowering wages.

    C. The demand curve would shift to the right, raising wages.

    D. The demand curve would shift to the left, lowering wages.

3. Which of the below graphs shows how demand-pull inflation occurs? _____

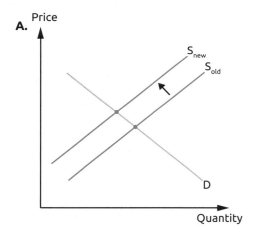

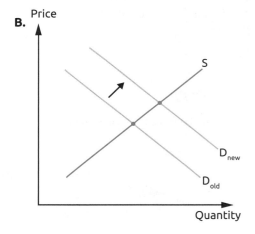

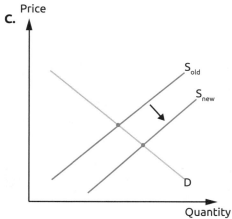

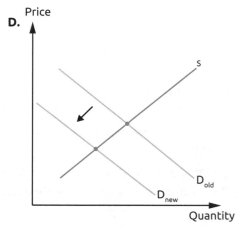

Unions and the Labor Market

The **labor market** is similar to other markets in certain ways. It obeys the Law of Supply and Demand. It's different because the demand for labor is a derived demand, and the supply of labor is affected by population growth, education, and immigration. There's another factor that affects the labor market: **unions**. A union is a group of workers who join together to increase their power in the labor market. Unions get involved in negotiating contracts with employers. These negotiations have an impact on wages and working conditions.

Unions use a variety of methods to benefit their members. Their main function is to engage in **collective bargaining**. This is the process by which employees, represented by their union leaders, negotiate with the employer. There's power in numbers, and the right to bargain collectively gives workers the ability to get better contracts from their employers. Unions also use **strikes** and **work slowdowns** to influence employers. In a strike, workers stop work to force an employer to agree to their demands. In a work slowdown, workers keep working, but at a slower rate.

The Rise and Decline of Unions

Unions fought hard to gain these rights. In 1935, Congress passed the **Wagner Act**. The Wagner Act gave unions the right to bargain collectively. It also made strikes legal and prevented employers from firing employees who were involved in unions. It created the National Labor Review Board to handle disputes between unions and employers. The Wagner Act was amended in 1947 by the **Taft-Hartley Act**. This law regulated the activities of unions and limited their power. It required unions to give 60 days' notice of an impending strike and outlawed the **closed shop.** A closed shop is a business in which employees must join a union before being hired.

Political and economic changes have hurt unions in recent decades. **Outsourcing** has sent many of the jobs once held by union members to other countries. As a result, union membership has declined a great deal since its peak in the mid-20th century. While unions have not disappeared from the U.S. labor market, the decreasing number of jobs in traditionally unionized areas like manufacturing, and increasing competition in a global economy, have both hurt unions. What role unions have to play in the future of the U.S. economy is uncertain, but their impact to this point has been significant.

Key Terms

closed shop

collective bargaining

labor market

outsourcing

strike

Taft-Hartley Act

union

Wagner Act

work slowdown

Skills Tip

Unions sound like they must be good for workers, but this a controversial claim. Collective bargaining brings higher wages, but higher wages aren't always beneficial in the long run. When wages are high, employers look to other countries to find workers who are willing to take lower wages. Some people believe that union power has resulted in outsourcing. Outsourcing usually hurts the very workers that unions are supposed to help.

Think about the connection between the rise of unions and the increase in outsourcing. Is the evidence for this connection compelling?

Complete the activities below to check your understanding of the lesson content. The Unit 4 Answer Key is on page 154.

Vocabulary

Complete each sentence below with one of the key terms below. Each term is used exactly once.

labor market	outsourcing	work slowdown	closed shop	collective bargaining

1. The Wagner Act gave unions the right to negotiate through _____.

2. The Taft-Hartley Act outlawed the _____.

3. A loss of jobs overseas is known as _____.

4. Workers who remain on the job can influence their employer through a _____.

5. A union is a group of workers who join together to increase their power in the _____.

Skills Practice

Choose the correct answer to each question.

6. What is the difference between the Taft-Hartley Act and the Wagner Act?

   A. The Taft-Hartley Act expanded union power more than the Wagner Act.

   B. The Taft-Hartley Act reduced the rights given to unions by the Wagner Act.

   C. The Taft-Hartley Act led to more strikes while the Wagner Act led to fewer strikes.

   D. The Taft-Hartley Act addressed outsourcing while the Wagner Act addressed collective bargaining.

7. Which statement accurately compares a work slowdown to a strike?

   A. A strike is done by a union while a work slowdown is done by an employer.

   B. A strike increases bargaining power while a work slowdown increases outsourcing.

   C. A strike is a legal method of influencing employers while a work slowdown is illegal.

   D. A strike involves workers leaving the job while a work slowdown keeps workers on the job.

8. Which of these has occurred in recent decades?

   A. Unions have gained more power.

   B. Unions have disappeared from the United States.

   C. Unions have lost a significant amount of their membership.

   D. Unions have abandoned the practice of collective bargaining.

Globalization

People and products can be flown to the other side of the world in less than day. Information and money can be transported around the globe instantly. This has created a high level of economic **interdependence** in today's world. Greater interdependence is a result of a process called **globalization**. Globalization has changed the way countries organize their economies. It has given rise to **international organizations** that promote **free trade**, which has no taxes or restrictions, and seek to protect themselves.

Trading Blocs and Economic Unions

Trade agreements are common in today's world. These agreements have created international organizations whose purpose is to grow the economies of member nations. The members of **trading blocs** agree to have free trade among their members. This means no **tariffs** (taxes) or other barriers to trade. The North American Free Trade Agreement (NAFTA) created a trading bloc made up of Canada, Mexico, and the United States. These nations **import** and **export** large amounts of goods between each other.

An **economic union** goes even further than a trading bloc. A union does not only eliminate **trade barriers,** but it also integrates the economies of its members. The European Union (EU) is an example of an economic union. The EU has created a **common market** among its members. There are no tariffs or other limits to trade among members, and they share policies protecting their economy as a whole. Many of the EU members also use the *euro* as their currency. The existence of a **common currency** increases efficiency and further promotes trade among members.

Key Terms

- cartel
- common currency
- common market
- economic union
- export
- free trade
- globalization
- import
- interdependence
- international organization
- international trade
- protectionism
- tariff
- trade agreement
- trade barrier
- trading bloc
- World Trade Organization

European Union (EU)

The European Union (EU) covers most, but not all, of the European continent. The formation of this trade union has eliminated economic borders. This has helped create one of the world's largest economies.

Free Trade and Protectionism

Vocabulary Tip

Connect key terms that are related to each other. An *economic union* is a type of international organization. So is a *cartel*. Making these kinds of connections makes it easier to remember important terms.

Globalization has increased the amount of **international trade**. It has also helped spread free trade policies. Supporters of free trade argue that trade barriers hurt the global economy. One important organization promoting free trade is the **World Trade Organization** (WTO), established in 1995. The WTO seeks to reduce or eliminate trade barriers. It tries to ensure that global trade is open, smooth, and predictable. The WTO's main function is to help members reach agreement on the rules for world trade. The WTO also helps resolve trade disputes.

However, there are still many limits on trade. Trade barriers are used by certain groups to benefit themselves. For example, a limit on the import of cars helps car companies and autoworkers. There are always groups pushing for protectionist policies that benefit themselves. Trading blocs and economic unions combine free trade policies with **protectionism**. They eliminate trade barriers among members, but they also create new barriers to block outside competition.

Cartels also limit free trade. A cartel is an organization that limits the supply of a particular good. This is done to keep prices high. It also protects a valuable resource. One of the most influential cartels in the world is the Organization of Petroleum Exporting Countries (OPEC). OPEC seeks to keep oil prices high by limiting the production of oil.

Skills Tip

Compare the information about OPEC shown on the map and the circle graph. Notice that OPEC's share of known oil reserves is extremely large, while the territory occupied by OPEC member nations is relatively small.

Members of the Organization of Petroleum Exporting Countries

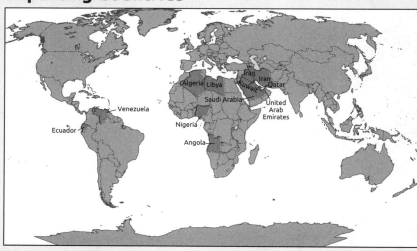

Known Oil Reserves

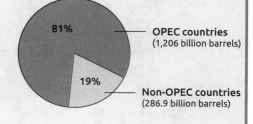

81% OPEC countries (1,206 billion barrels)

19% Non-OPEC countries (286.9 billion barrels)

Members of OPEC control a large majority of the world's known oil reserves. This give them a significant amount of power over global oil prices.

Complete the activities below to check your understanding of the lesson content. The Unit 4 Answer Key is on page 154.

Vocabulary

Complete each sentence below with one of the key terms from the box. Each term is used exactly once.

cartel	common market	free trade	globalization
international trade	protectionism	trade barrier	trading bloc

1. Canada, Mexico, and the United States make up a(n) _____

2. OPEC is an example of a(n) _____

3. An economic union has a _____

4. A tariff is a type of _____

5. Imports and exports are both types of _____

6. The opposite of free trade is _____

7. The World Trade Organization and NAFTA are both committed to _____

8. Greater interdependence is largely a result of _____

Answer the questions based on the content covered in this unit. The Unit 4 Answer Key is on page 154.

List the three basic economic questions and give an example of an individual or group answering each question.

1. Economic question _____
   _____

   Example: _____
   _____

2. Economic question _____
   _____

   Example: _____
   _____

3. Economic question _____
   _____

   Example: _____
   _____

Use the scenario below to answer questions 4–6.

Alicia has just graduated from high school. She is considering three options for her future:

- **Option 1:** Borrowing $20,000 from a bank to attend college.

- **Option 2:** Accepting a high-paying job with her parents' T-shirt company.

- **Option 3:** Accepting a low-paying job with a publishing company in New York City.

Alicia wants to be a writer someday. She would major in literature if she attended college. She believes that she would rise fast in the publishing company if she took that job. She has never been interested in getting involved in the T-shirt industry.

4. If Alicia chooses Option 3, the benefit she could have gained by choosing either of the other options is known as the

   A. labor pool.

   B. supply shock.

   C. opportunity cost.

   D. quantity demanded.

5. Alicia cannot choose all three options because she has

   A. a scarcity of time.

   B. a high derived demand.

   C. already maximized her utility.

   D. allocated her resources efficiently.

6. Which statement *best* explains why the job with the publishing company pays less than the job with the T-shirt company?

   A. The publishing company makes a larger profit than the T-shirt company.

   B. There are more people willing to take the job with the publishing company.

   C. There are fewer people qualified to do the job with the publishing company.

   D. The T-shirt company is in an industry with a higher derived demand for its products.

Use the scenario to answer questions 7–10.

Magnus is a glass blower whose work is relatively unknown, but then his fancy water glasses are shown in a national magazine. The diagram below shows the various stages Magnus's business goes through as a result of the magazine article.

Stage 1
- Within days of the magazine coming out, every glass collector in the country wants one of Magnus's fancy water glasses.

Stage 2
- Three months later, Magnus is unable to keep up with orders. He hires ten workers to produce water glasses based on his design. He can now make ten times as many glasses as he did when he was working alone.

Stage 3
- After a year, nearly every collector has one of Magnus's water glasses, so orders drop off to almost nothing. Magnus continues to employ his ten new workers.

Stage 4
- Ten years later, Magnus's fancy water glasses are in fashion again. However, Magnus fired all of his workers and quit making glass. He's a painter now. Many of the glasses made ten years earlier got broken as they were being used, so now very few are left.

7. At which stage will the price for Magnus's water glasses be highest?

   A. 1

   B. 2

   C. 3

   D. 4

8. Which of these is *most likely* to happen during Stage 3?

   A. Magnus begins losing money.

   B. Magnus raises his workers' pay.

   C. Magnus experiences record profits.

   D. Magnus popularity as an artist grows.

9. At Stage 4, there is a(n)

   A. shortage.

   B. supply shock.

   C. derived demand.

   D. opportunity cost.

10. Draw a supply and demand graph that shows what happens at Stage 2.

POSTTEST

Answer these questions to see how well you have learned the social studies content and skills in this book.

1. As the American real estate market boomed in the early 2000s, which of the following was also taking place?

   A. The Internet was becoming popular.

   B. Al-Qaeda was planning an invasion of Iraq.

   C. Individuals and groups were making risky investments.

   D. Obamacare was being implemented.

2. Which was an effect of the increased immigration to the United States in the late 1800s?

   A. urbanization

   B. industrialization

   C. segregation

   D. revolution

3. Which of the following is NOT found in the U.S. Constitution?

   A. the structure of the federal government

   B. the powers of each branch of the federal government

   C. reasons for fighting the American Revolution

   D. amendments to the Constitution

4. A person in favor of stronger labor unions would support which of the following?

   A. increasing outsourcing

   B. weakening the Taft-Hartley Act

   C. outlawing work stoppages

   D. abolishing the National Labor Review Board

5. A historian arguing that World War II could have been prevented would most likely base the argument on the failure of which policy?

   A. nuclear deterrence

   B. alliance building

   C. the New Deal

   D. appeasement

6. Which of these events had the most direct impact on fighting the effects of the Great Depression?

   A. World War I

   B. speculation on the stock market

   C. the Zimmerman Telegram

   D. the New Deal

7. Which of the following scenarios is NOT an example of checks and balances?

   A. a presidential veto of a bill passed by Congress

   B. the Supreme Court's ruling an act of Congress unconstitutional

   C. a presidential pardon of a convicted criminal

   D. the Senate's rejection of a presidential nomination

8. Which of the following had a great impact on denying African Americans their civil rights?

   A. "Black codes"

   B. The Fifteenth Amendment

   C. The *Brown* v. *Board of Education* decision

   D. The Fourteenth Amendment

9. Which of the following actions is prohibited because states are bound by the "full faith and credit" clause in the Constitution?

   A. A state issues a new driver's license to a citizen who just moved within its borders.

   B. A state legislature changes a marriage law to match a neighboring state's.

   C. A state arrests a person suspected of committing a crime in another state.

   D. An individual files a new lawsuit in an attempt to obtain a more favorable outcome on a matter that has already been decided.

140

10. Following the French and Indian War, what was the colonists' main complaint with the British government?

   A. The British government was boycotting American-made goods.

   B. The British king was forcing American colonists to move farther west.

   C. The colonies were being taxed, yet they had no representation in the British Parliament.

   D. Parliament opened up colonial lands in the east to Native American groups.

11. Which of the following is NOT an example of a formal geographic region?

   A. Europe

   B. the Rust Belt

   C. the Sahara Desert

   D. Texas

12. An economic union looking to integrate its members' economies and increase economic activity would probably consider which of the following policies?

   A. adopting a common currency

   B. implementing trade barriers among member countries

   C. initiating protectionism policies within the union

   D. breaking off all economic ties to other trade blocs and organizations

13. An American critic of communist governments would likely argue that communism deprives individuals of which democratic ideal?

   A. the right to an attorney if charged with a crime

   B. the right to join a militia

   C. the right to life, liberty, and the pursuit of happiness

   D. the right to purchase goods

14. Which of the following was a political idea formed by the ancient Greeks?

   A. democracy   C. imperialism

   B. reformism   D. communism

15. The process of helping the South recover from the war and bringing African Americans into American society was called _____.

   A. emancipation   C. states' rights

   B. secession   D. reconstruction

16. Which statement best describes a key difference between the Northern and Southern military capabilities in the Civil War?

   A. The North had fewer soldiers but more weapons than the South.

   B. The South had more efficient transport systems, but the North had more trains.

   C. The South had fewer soldiers but better military commanders than the North.

   D. The North had better morale while many Southerners did not believe in the war.

17. The Missouri Compromise maintained a balance of power between the North and South by

   A. allowing slavery in all new states that joined the Union.

   B. splitting Missouri into two slave states.

   C. allowing slavery in no portion of the Louisiana Territory.

   D. adding a slave state and a free state to the Union at the same time.

Complete each sentence with the correct answer.

18. According to the Declaration of Independence, citizens of a country have the right to _____ if their natural rights are taken away.

19. A law, rule, or regulation made and enforced by a city government is called a _____

Complete each sentence with one of the terms listed. Use each term one time.

inflation	median	wages
demand-pull inflation	cost-push inflation	

20. _____ is caused by a rise in production costs.

21. _____ is the continued increase in the price of goods and services.

22. An increase in prices driven by rising consumer demand is called _____.

23. The _____ is a way of showing the center of a statistical dataset.

24. The prices paid for labor services provided are called _____.

Complete each sentence with one of the terms listed. Use each term one time.

Inca	Maya	adobe
Aztec	Iroquois Confederacy	

25. From the city of Tenochtitlan, the _____ ruled a large empire.

26. The Pueblo built structures made of _____ bricks.

27. Group decision-making and war pacts were features of the _____.

28. The _____ lived along the western coast of South America.

29. Architecture and astronomy were areas of expertise of the _____.

Questions 30 and 31 refer to the following political cartoon and information.

This political cartoon is titled *Southern Ideas of Liberty*. It criticizes attempts in the South to suppress abolitionism. A judge with donkey ears and a whip sits on bales of cotton. Beneath his feet is the Constitution. He is sentencing an abolitionist to be lynched.

30. In which region of the country was this cartoon most likely published?

   A. the South

   B. undecided territories in the west

   C. the North

   D. states that bordered the North and South

31. What is the cartoonist's point of view of those who oppose abolitionism?

   _____

32. What limits are placed on the freedom of speech?

   _____

Complete each sentence with one of the terms listed. Use each term one time.

soft money	hard money	initiative
Electoral College	Political Action Committee	

33. The _____ is the group of state representatives that officially chooses the president.

34. _____ is campaign donations that are used for general election purposes.

35. A(n) _____ is an organization working to get a certain candidate elected.

36. Citizens can propose new laws through the election process called a(n) _____.

37. Campaign money given directly to a candidate is called _____.

Read the following passage, and then answer questions 38 and 39.

"The accumulation of all powers, legislative, executive, and judiciary, in the same hands, whether of one, a few, or many, and whether hereditary, self-appointed, or elective, may justly be pronounced the very definition of tyranny."

—James Madison, *The Federalist, No. 10.*

38. In this passage, Madison is arguing for which constitutional principle?

   A. a bill of rights

   B. separation of powers

   C. checks and balances

   D. popular sovereignty

39. Which statement best summarizes Madison's view on governmental power?

   A. Too much power in the hands of one person or group leads to tyranny.

   B. Not all abuses of government power are bad.

   C. Elected officials are justified in accumulating all powers.

   D. Hereditary power leads to democracy.

Read the following passage, and then answer questions 40–42.

Governments, organizations, and individuals are all working to control pollution. People can and should recycle. Recycling is sending garbage to be reused as a new item. The U.S. government created the Environmental Protection Agency (EPA) in the 1970s. This agency monitors air and water pollution. People are also turning to renewable energy resources like wind and solar power. These do not create pollution.

40. Which of the following is the author's main conclusion?

   A. Governments and individuals are working to control pollution.

   B. Renewable resources are not helpful in controlling pollution.

   C. Recycling is the only effective practice that can control pollution.

   D. The U.S. government has not done enough to control pollution.

41. Which of the following is an opinion offered by the passage?

   A. The U.S. government created the Environmental Protection Agency (EPA) in the 1970s.

   B. Recycling is sending garbage to be reused as a new item.

   C. People can and should recycle.

   D. People are also turning to renewable energy resources like wind and solar power.

42. The information in the passage supports which of the following conclusions?

    A. Recycling has not been effective.

    B. The EPA requires more power to control pollution.

    C. Solar power is much better than wind power.

    D. Controlling pollution requires the efforts of both individuals and governments.

Read the following passage, and then answer questions 43 and 44.

"The economic order or local economic activities in any country are built up over long years and reflect the influence of each country's traditions, habits, and national lifestyles. However, globalism progressed without any regard for various non-economic values, nor for environmental issues or problems of resource restriction. If we look back on the changes in Japanese society that have occurred since the end of the Cold War, I believe it is no exaggeration to say that the global economy has damaged traditional economic activities and destroyed local communities."

—Yukio Hatoyama, former prime minister of Japan

43. Which of the following is Hatoyama's main complaint about globalization?

    A. Only small, local communities have prospered from globalism.

    B. Globalization has damaged Japanese society and culture.

    C. Japan has not benefited economically from globalization.

    D. Globalization has taken too long to reach Japan.

44. Based on Hatoyama's statements in the passage, which of the following best describes the foundation of Japanese economic strength?

    A. traditional local economic activities

    B. non-traditional values

    C. the influence of outside ideas on Japanese habits

    D. economic flexibility

Read the following passage, and then answer questions 45–47.

"What stronger evidence can be given of the want of energy in our governments than these disorders? If there exists not a power to check them, what security has a man for life, liberty, or property? . . . the consequences of a lax, or inefficient government, are too obvious to be dwelt on. Thirteen sovereignties pulling against each other, and all tugging at the federal head will soon bring ruin on the whole; whereas a liberal, and energetic Constitution, well guarded and closely watched, to prevent incroachments, might restore us to that degree of respectability and consequence. . . ."

—from George Washington's letter to James Madison, November 5, 1786

45. Based on this excerpt, what is Washington's view of the current government?

    A. It is too strong and is crushing local governments.

    B. It is too weak to be effective.

    C. It needs a few minor adjustments to make it work.

    D. It provides too many rights to citizens.

46. What, according to Washington, will cause the ruin of the government?

    A. protesters and many small rebellions that cannot be controlled

    B. states that act in too much independence from the federal government

    C. the inability of the federal government to protect the rights of life, liberty, and property

    D. the thirteen states' fighting among themselves and demanding too much of the federal government

144

47. Which of the following best summarizes Washington's main recommendation to fix the current government?

   A. Create a new, stronger constitution and government that have limits and are monitored.

   B. Revise the current system, but add more laws to protect basic civil rights.

   C. Grant more power to state governments to relieve pressure on the federal government.

   D. Reduce the power of the state governments and grant unlimited powers to the federal government.

Read the following passage, and then answer questions 48–50.

> The American colonies grew rapidly in the early 1700s. After England defeated France in the French and Indian War (1754–1763), England took over many of France's North American colonies. Victory against France then motivated England to seek greater control of its colonies. England also had to recover from the huge debts caused by the war. England then imposed new taxes and policies that led to conflict between the British government and the colonists.

48. How did Great Britain solidify its power in North America in the 1700s?

   _____

   _____

   _____

49. Which key events or conditions in the 1700s altered the political makeup of North America?

   _____

   _____

   _____

50. What was the effect of Britain's actions in North America in the 1700s?

   _____

   _____

   _____

Match each term on the left with its definition on the right.

51.	utility	A.	buying and selling things
52.	voluntary exchange	B.	what you give up when you make a decision
53.	scarcity	C.	how useful a person finds a particular good or service
54.	opportunity cost	D.	having wants and needs that are greater than what is available

Match each term on the left with its definition on the right.

55.	*Common Sense*	A.	protest against British laws
56.	Boston Tea Party	B.	American colonists who supported the British
57.	loyalists	C.	British tax on colonial printed materials
58.	Stamp Act	D.	influential pamphlet advocating American independence

Match each amendment with its chief purpose.

59.	Tenth Amendment	A.	establishes the right of Americans to own firearms
60.	First Amendment	B.	protects the rights of citizens accused of crimes
61.	Fifth Amendment	C.	reserves some powers to the state governments
62.	Second Amendment	D.	protects Americans' civil liberties

Match each term on the left with its definition on the right.

63.	continent	A.	imaginary horizontal lines around the earth
64.	longitude	B.	central line of longitude around the earth
65.	latitude	C.	imaginary vertical lines around the earth
66.	Prime Meridian	D.	large landmass on Earth

Match each cause on the left with its effect.

Causes	Effects

Causes

67. The Byzantine Empire fell

68. Mongols kept roads and provinces safe

69. Islam founder Muhammad died

70. China loosened economic rules

Effects

A. trade thrived in Asia and eastern Europe

B. China became one of the world's most powerful economies

C. Muslims split into two competing sects

D. the Ottoman Empire emerged

Use the map to answer questions 71–73.

Coronado National Forest

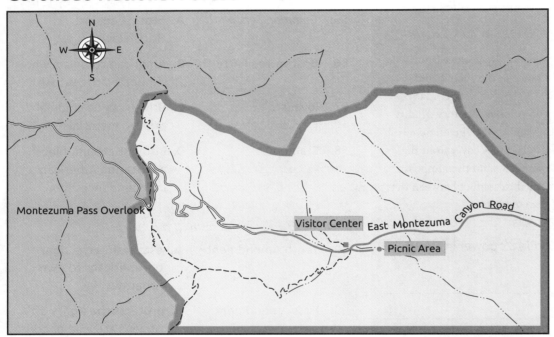

71. What is the name of the only paved road in Coronado National Forest?

_____

72. Which direction would you head to reach Montezuma Pass Overlook from the Visitor Center?

_____

73. How many picnic areas are located within Coronado National Forest?

_____

Use the following information to answer questions 74–76.

Population Pyramids of California

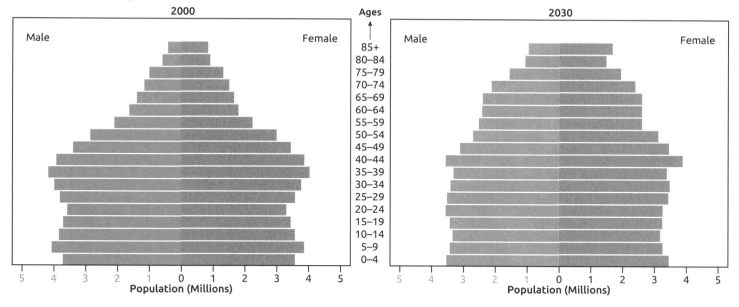

74. What age groups have the highest population in 2000? _____

75. How is the population of females 85+ projected to change by 2030? _____

76. What general conclusion can you make based on the change in the shape of the pyramid from 2000 to 2030?

_____

_____

Study the data set. Then, complete the sentences with the correct answer.

Chicago Precipitation												
	Jan	**Feb**	**Mar**	**Apr**	**May**	**Jun**	**Jul**	**Aug**	**Sep**	**Oct**	**Nov**	**Dec**
Inches of rain	2	2	3	3	4	3	4	5	3	3	3	2
Inches of snow	11	9	6	1	0	0	0	0	0	1	1	9

77. The average amount of rain in Chicago for the months of March, April, and May is _____ inches.

78. The median amount of snow in Chicago for the months of December, January, February, March, and April is _____ inches.

Read the following quotation, and then answer questions 79–81. The quotation is from a televised speech by President Lyndon B. Johnson on the night of July 2, 1964. In the speech, President Johnson explained the Civil Rights Act of 1964.

"I am about to sign into law the Civil Rights Act of 1964. I want to take this occasion to talk to you about what that law means to every American. . . . We believe that all men are created equal. Yet many are denied equal treatment.

We believe that all men have certain unalienable rights. Yet many Americans do not enjoy those rights. . . . We believe that all men are entitled to the blessings of liberty. Yet millions are being deprived of those blessings—not because of their own failures, but because of the color of their skin. . . .

The purpose of the law is simple.

It does not restrict the freedom of any American, so long as he respects the rights of others.

It does not give special treatment to any citizen. It does say the only limit to a man's hope for happiness, and for the future of his children, shall be his own ability."

79. How does Johnson remind listeners of key democratic principles?

   A. He mentions the destruction caused during the Civil War.

   B. He quotes certain parts of the Bill of Rights.

   C. He refers to parts of the Declaration of Independence and American ideals.

   D. He describes the struggles of civil rights activists.

80. According to Johnson, why are many Americans denied equal rights?

   A. because of their personal failures

   B. because of the color of their skin

   C. because Americans refuse to provide special treatment to certain groups

   D. because the Constitution, as written, does not grant equal rights to *all* citizens

81. Which phrase best shows Johnson's support of equality for all Americans?

   A. "It does not give special treatment to any citizen."

   B. "It does not restrict the freedom of any American."

   C. "The only limit to a man's hope for happiness, and for the future of his children, shall be his own ability."

   D. ". . .so long as he respects the rights of others."

Use the following information to answer questions 82 and 83.

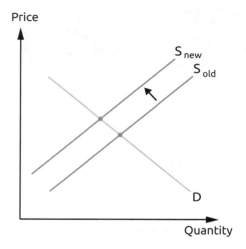

82. Which of the following conclusions is supported by the graph?

   A. Quantity has increased.

   B. Both supply and demand have dropped.

   C. Supply has decreased.

   D. The price has dropped.

83. Which of the following statements best explains the changes on the graph?

   A. The market equilibrium price went up because of a supply shock.

   B. High prices lead to higher demand.

   C. Consumers are more willing to pay higher prices.

   D. A drop in supply leads to lower prices.

POSTTEST ANSWER KEY

1. C.

2. A. With the increase of people moving to the United States, living space needed to be created.

3. C. Reasons for fighting the Revolutionary War can be found in the Declaration of Independence, where Americans stated their grievances with English rule.

4. B.

5. D. Appeasement was the policy stating that if the Allies let Hitler invade Poland, he would stop there. Allies let the invasion of Poland happen but instead of stopping, Hitler triggered World War II.

6. D. The New Deal started government programs like Social Security to help boost the economy.

7. C.

8. A.

9. D. Once a court makes a decision, it is upheld in all courts across the country.

10. C.

11. B.

12. A. When countries have a common currency, it boosts the economy of each country.

13. C.

14. A.

15. D.

16. D.

17. D. The balance continued because two states were admitted to the United States. The numbers between free and slave states stayed the same.

18. form a new government

19. municipal ordinance

20. cost-push inflation

21. inflation

22. demand-pull inflation

23. median

24. wages

25. Aztec

26. adobe

27. Iroquois Confederacy

28. Inca

29. Maya

30. C. Because the cartoon is criticizing the South, one can assume it was published in the North.

31. Sample answer: The cartoonist has a very negative opinion of the anti-abolitionists. Based on the drawing, the cartoonist thinks the anti-abolitionists are lawless and do not respect the U.S. Constitution.

32. Sample answer: Americans cannot use their free speech rights to limit the rights and freedoms of others. They also cannot use speech intended to cause violence or public disruptions.

33. Electoral College

34. soft money

35. Political Action Committee

36. initiative

37. hard money

38. B. Think of which term most aligns with the idea that one person should not have all of the power a government has.

39. A.

40. A.

41. C.

42. D. Look for the option that best encompasses the point of the passage.

43. B.

44. A.

45. B. If the states have too many rights, the federal government might be weakened.

46. D. If states have too much power, there might be no part of the government that can check them.

47. A.

48. Sample answer: Britain solidified its power by growing its colonies and by defeating France in the French and Indian War.

49. Sample answer: England's colonies grew rapidly, giving it more and more power. England then was able to defeat France. The American colonists lost power and influence when England taxed the colonists.

50. Sample answer: England's actions first led to war with France. Its tax and economic policies led to tension between the government and the colonists.

51. C.
52. A.
53. D.
54. B.
55. D.
56. A.
57. B.
58. C.
59. C.
60. D.
61. B.
62. A.
63. D.
64. C.
65. A.
66. B.
67. D.
68. A.
69. C.
70. B.

71. East Montezuma Canyon Road

72. west

73. 1

74. 35–39

75. Sample answer: That population will double by 2030.

76. Sample answer: The U.S. population is getting older.

77. 3.33

78. 9
79. C.
80. B.
81. A.
82. C.
83. A.

After checking your Posttest answers using the Answer Key, use the chart below to find the questions you did not answer correctly. Then locate the pages in this book where you can review the content needed to answer those questions correctly.

Question	Where to Look for Help		
	Unit	Lesson	Page
1	2	10	70
2	2	7	60
3, 45, 46, 47	2	4	50
4	4	4	133
5, 6	2	8	63
7	3	5	94
8, 80	3	9	106
9	3	6	98
10, 48, 49, 50, 55, 56, 57, 58, 79	2	3	47
11	1	2	16
12, 43, 44	4	5	135
13, 18	3	2	81
14, 38, 39	3	1	77
15, 16, 35, 36	2	6	57
17, 30, 31	2	5	54
19	3	7	101
20, 21, 22, 23, 24	4	3	130
25, 26, 27, 28, 29	2	1	39
32, 59, 60, 61, 62	3	3	85
33, 34, 35, 36, 37	3	10	109
40, 41, 42	1	4	23
51, 52, 53, 54	4	1	123
63, 64, 65, 66	1	2	17–18
67, 68, 69, 70	1	8	34
71, 72, 73	1	1	12
74, 75, 76	1	3	20
77, 78	1	5	26
81	2	9	66
82, 83	4	2	127

ANSWER KEY

Unit 1: Geography and the World

Lesson 1: Geography and Geographic Tools

1. D.
2. F.
3. A.
4. E.
5. B.
6. C.
7. This is a political map. I can tell because it shows cities and borders.
8. Large cities include St. Louis, Kansas City, Independence, and Springfield.
9. This map is missing the scale. The scale helps users tell real distances between places.
10. Sample answer: I could add information showing the places where Native Americans had settlements before American settlers arrived.

Lesson 2: Global and U.S. Regions

1. large landmass
2. one-half of Earth
3. imaginary lines encircling Earth horizontally
4. imaginary line of longitude separating the Eastern and Western Hemispheres
5. an area that has a shared characteristic
6. perceptual
7. formal
8. perceptual
9. functional
10. formal
11. perceptual
12.

Physical Outline

13.

Physical Outline

14. These imaginary lines divide the hemispheres. They are the center lines of measurement for latitude and longitude.

Lesson 3: Studying Populations

1. C.
2. B.
3. The largest group is people age 10–14. The next highest is people age 15–19.
4. Sample answer: I predict that the population will grow over time. The birth rate seems high, and most children reach adulthood. They will probably survive to have more children and grow the population.
5. Sample answer: People probably have access to at least some health care throughout their lives. People who reach adulthood usually live for a while. But care for older people is not as good. Treatment for diseases like heart disease and cancer is probably hard to access.

Lesson 4: Natural Resources and Pollution

1. resource made of carbon and formed underground
2. harmful thing in the environment
3. resource that can regrown or be reused
4. visible air pollution
5. D.
6. A.
7. Sample answer: Air pollution happens when people release harmful substances into the air. Factories or cars pollute by burning fossil fuels. This adds dirty substances to air and can lead to smog.
8. Sample answer: Water pollution happens when rivers, streams, lakes, or oceans become dirty. Factories can release waste into water. Air pollution can lead to water pollution when clouds gather polluted air and send it to Earth as rain.

Lesson 5: Climate and Weather

1. D.
2. A.
3. F.
4. E.
5. C.
6. B.
7. 87.6
8. 38
9. 71

Lesson 6: Globalization

1. interconnectedness of people, ideas, and economies around the world
2. systems like roads and power lines
3. spread of U.S. popular culture worldwide
4. company that operates worldwide
5. Sample answer: President Carter argues that globalization benefits some people but not everyone. He especially thinks globalization does not help people in poor countries. I agree with his argument. People in poor countries do not always have access to good infrastructure. They often make low wages. They cannot get the goods traded around the world brought to them. They cannot afford them, either. Multinational corporations open factories in poor parts of the world. But they may not pay their employees well. So the benefits of globalization are mostly for people who are already in rich countries.

Lesson 7: Turning Points in World History—The West

1. system of government in which citizens vote on laws and leaders
2. taking control of other countries as colonies
3. time of new interest in art and ideas
4. time of new interest in reason and observation

9	8	5	7	10	6

11. A.
12. C.

Lesson 8: Turning Points in World History—The East

1. Quran
2. dynasties
3. communism
4. cultural diffusion
5. B.
6. D.
7. D.
8. A, C.
9. B.

Unit Practice Test

1.

Functional Region	Perceptual Region
B usually centered on a city	A vary based on a person's ideas
D typical of metropolitan areas	E have often-changing boundaries
F may be administered as a political unit	C are not used formally

2. D. People coming into the country or leaving the country in large numbers would greatly affect the population growth.

3. C.

4. D. It is written in the first person, signaling that the text represents the speaker's thoughts.

5. D.

6. 78.3.

7. 55.5.

8. 64.

9. A.

10. C.

11. C. Option B can be quickly eliminated because Rome is in Europe, not Asia.

Unit 2: U.S. History

Lesson 1: The Americas Before 1492

1. dried mud used to make bricks

2. person who survives by hunting animals and gathering crops

3. system to bring water to crops

4. historical area in Mexico and Central America

5. Inca

6. Maya

7. Sample answer: I think it was created by a person who lived in Mesoamerica long ago.

8. Sample answer: The illustration seems to show adults helping children enter a building. It may be students entering a school.

9. Sample answer: Many figures representing children are included in this illustration. This means it is likely about a topic related to children.

10. Sample answer: I think it was created to help show others what life was like in Mesoamerica. The creator may have wanted to show that the civilization cared about educating its children.

Lesson 2: European Colonization

1. D.

2. A.

3. Middle

4. Southern

5. Southern

6. New England

7. New England

8. Middle

9. Sample answer: Event 1. Anne Hutchinson settles in Boston; Event 2. Anne Hutchinson gives talks about religion; Event 3. Anne Hutchinson is expelled from Boston; Event 4. Anne Hutchinson helps found Rhode Island

Lesson 3: The American Revolution

1. C.

2. A.

3. E.

4. B.

5. F.

6. D.

7. B.

8. C.

Lesson 4: Founding a New Nation

1. Articles of Confederation

2. Bill of Rights

3. Cabinet

4. Northwest Ordinance

5. The author believes that they are bad and should be avoided.

6. Factions can be avoided in two ways. The two ways are ending liberty and making people think the same way.

7. Ending liberty to avoid factions is not worth it. Liberty is more important than avoiding factions.

8. The author says liberty "is essential to political life" just like air is to animal life. Getting rid of liberty is just as bad as getting rid of air because the things it supports die.

Lesson 5: Expansion and Sectionalism

1. someone who wanted to end slavery

2. In 1803, France sold the United States a huge chunk of land along the Mississippi River.

3. voting on whether to allow slavery in a place

4. support for the needs of one's own region over any others

5. Missouri Compromise

6. manifest destiny

7. John O'Sullivan wrote this document in 1845.

8. Most Americans in the mid-1800s supported westward expansion. They thought the nation had a duty to spread to the Pacific Ocean.

9. The author's point of view is that the nation must expand westward to fulfill its "manifest destiny" and have enough room for its growing population.

10. Sample answer: A Native American living in the West would probably have disagreed with the author. Native Americans' context was different because they lost their lands when new settlers came in to live on them. Westward expansion was a threat to them rather than a benefit, as it was to the author.

Lesson 6: Civil War and Reconstruction

1. B.

2. C.

3.

Causes of the Civil War	Effects of the Civil War
idea of states' rights	new public schools
disagreements over slavery	Thirteenth Amendment
election of Lincoln	military governors in the South

4. Sample answers: we here highly resolve that these dead shall not have died in vain; government of the people, by the people, for the people shall not perish from the earth.

5. Sample answer: The people who have died fighting in the war were protecting the U.S. government and its ideals.

ANSWER KEY

Lesson 7: Industrialization and Reform

1. blend into
2. ballot measure suggested by the public
3. place where immigrants could get help
4. growth of cities
5. Transcontinental Railroad
6. recall
7. A.
8. C.

Lesson 8: A World at War

1. D.
2. C.
3. B.
4. A.
5. F.
6. E.
7.

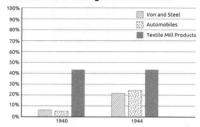

Women as Percentage of All Workers

Iron and Steel
Automobiles
Textile Mill Products

Lesson 9: Realizing Democratic Ideals

1. time of competition between the United States and the Soviet Union
2. belief in women's rights
3. laws that allowed segregation and unfair treatment
4. country with a lot of influence around the world
5. It is a dream deeply rooted in the American dream; rise up and live out the true meaning of its creed: "We hold these truths to be self-evident, that all men are created equal."
6. the sons of former slaves and the sons of former slave owners will be able to sit down together at the table of brotherhood
7. Sample answer: They will be able to have freedom and equality.
8. Sample answer: There will be no more racism. People will judge one another for their actions and not their race.

Lesson 10: The United States Today

1. B.
2. E.
3. A.
4. D.
5. C.
6. F.
7. A.
8. C.

Unit Practice Test

1. D.
2. B.
3. A.
4. D. Amendments are additions to a legal document. The Bill of Rights included ten amendments to the Constitution, which were intended to improve and uphold democratic ideals.
5. C.
6. A. Reread the passages on the Civil Rights and abolitionist movements, and see which of the options are true for both.
7. Civil War
8. C. *Unaffiliated* means that someone/ something is not officially connected with an organization or group.
9. B.
10. Kentucky
11. A. A lasting impression would mean that the implemented programs lasted a long time.
12.

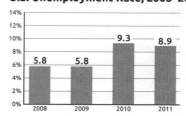

U.S. Unemployment Rate, 2008–2011

13. D.
14. A. King explains that he has tried a nonviolent campaign, but it is not working.
15. D.
16. C. King is referring to the police using nonviolence to defend segregation.

Lesson 1: Roots of U.S. Democracy

1. H.
2. F.
3. G.
4. C.
5. D.
6. A.
7. B.
8. E.
9. John Locke and Charles de Secondat, Baron de Montesquieu wrote these documents. Locke's document was written first, in 1691.
10. Locke believed that commonwealths (governments) were the best way to protect one's property.
11. Montesquieu is writing in support of the idea of separation of powers.
12. Sample answer: Both Locke and Montesquieu think that governments can offer protection and security to its citizens. Locke is concerned with the protection of property, and Montesquieu writes that properly organized governments can provide safety and liberty.

Lesson 2: Foundational Documents

1. the beginning of a document, like the Declaration of Independence
2. main parts or sections of the U.S. Constitution that describe important information
3. a branch of the government that makes laws; also known as Congress
4. one of the founders of the United States; the main writer of the Declaration of Independence
5. Government power comes from the people, who agree to follow the government.
6. Sample answer: The ideas in the Constitution make it clear that it is the people who have created the Constitution and the government. Like the Declaration, the Constitution states that the real power of government comes from the citizens.

Lesson 3: Bill of Rights

1. Due process
2. federal
3. searches and seizures
4. civil liberties
5. Franklin thinks that free speech helps support free government. He also states that some governments are stronger because people are free to question and examine them.
6. Sample answer: Yes. Franklin's support of free speech makes me think he would have been a supporter of other freedoms as well. I think he would have believed that civil liberties help create a free society.

Lesson 4: Three Branches of Government

1. judicial review
2. foreign policy
3. separation of powers
4. Cabinet
5. Congress
6. executive
7. legislative
8. judicial
9. executive
10. legislative
11. judicial
12. The cartoon suggests that the executive and legislative branches are in conflict with each other.
13. Each branch of government has specific powers and responsibilities. Congress believed Nixon was becoming too powerful, so it investigated his administration. The judicial branch (Supreme Court) did its job and gave Congress the power to check the president.

Lesson 5: Balancing Power

1. system of government that shares power between the federal government and the states
2. powers that both state and federal governments have
3. to accuse a government official of wrongdoing
4. legislation being considered, before becoming law
5. a set of laws or policies a president hopes to pass
6. to reject a bill

7. D.
8. B.
9. A.
10. Sample answer: This is an example of checks and balances because the executive branch has the power to accept or reject Congress's bills. Congress can override the president if two-thirds of both houses support the bill.
11. Sample answer: These rules force Congress and the president to be involved in making laws so that both branches know what is going on. Each branch can check and balance the other to try to make sure that only good bills make it into law.

Lesson 6: State Governments

1. infrastructure
2. full faith and credit
3. republican
4. federal
5. state
6. federal
7. state
8. federal
9. state

Lesson 7: Municipal Governments

1. D.
2. A.
3. B.
4. E.
5. C.
6. county
7. special district
8. municipal
9. townships

Lesson 8: Citizenship

1. the process required to become a citizen
2. actions that help everyone
3. respect for the rights and opinions of others
4. actions that citizens are expected to do
5. actions that citizens are required by law to do
6. Sample answers: has been summoned; national loyalty; answered the call to service; ask what you can do for your country

7. Kennedy thinks all American citizens have an important role to play. He says that citizens and not the president will determine the success or failure of the country. Also, he states that citizens should reach out and find ways to help.

Lesson 9: Expanding Rights

1. Seneca Falls Convention
2. discrimination
3. women's rights movement
4. black codes
5. suffrage
6. This section focuses on state government.
7. Sample answer: States had found ways to get around following the amendments in the Bill of Rights. Only a Constitutional amendment could stop states from restricting its citizens' rights.

Lesson 10: Political Parties, Campaigns, and Elections

1. Federal Election Commission
2. Electoral College
3. hard money
4. convention
5. Madison believes political parties are bad.
6. Madison lists many different ways in which political parties would divide different groups of citizens.
7. Strong political parties that unite large numbers of people could limit the rights of the minority.

Lesson 11: Landmark Supreme Court Decisions

1. when a law is reversed
2. part of the Fourteenth Amendment that guarantees equal treatment
3. when a law is agreed with and ruled constitutional
4. a list of rights that must be read to suspects when they are taken into police custody
5. *Miranda* v. *Arizona*
6. *Brown* v. *Board of Education*
7. *Plessey* v. *Ferguson*
8. *Roe* v. *Wade*
9. *Gideon* v. *Wainwright*
10. *Dred Scott* v. *Stanford*

ANSWER KEY

Lesson 12: Controversies in Politics

1. Affordable Care Act
2. DREAMers
3. dark money
4. bias
5. B.
6. D.
7. C.
8. B.
9. Reagan viewed government as not very effective in solving problems. He seems to think that the people are more capable of governing than a small group of politicians who run the government.
10. Sample answer: Reagan's negative opinion of government leads me to think that he would favor a small, limited federal government.

Unit Practice Test

1. C.
2. D. It might be helpful to list different levels in order of importance and note the main responsibility of each.
3. A.
4. B. Look for the tone in the passage. Aside from the information, try to identify what the speaker wants to get across.
5. C. The colonists' decision to form their own government and gain their independence also means that they had to separate from English rule.
6.

Legislative	Executive	Judicial
write the nation's laws	serve as commander in chief	decide whether federal laws are constitutional
control the nation's taxing and spending	appoint ambassadors	consider constitutional rights cases
impeach government officials	develop foreign policy	ensure laws are justly enforced

7. B.
8. A. Revisit the section on checks and balances.
9. D.

10.C. Think about which option implies that she would experience more difficulty than others.
11. D. Based on the previous question, think about which option best represents her views and obstacles.
12. A.
13. A. Revisit Lesson 11 and review the landmark Supreme Court decisions. Look for how many of the decisions pertain to race.
14. C.

Unit 4: Economics

Lesson 1: Basic Economic Questions

1. decide how to use a resource
2. a lack of something
3. what you give up when you make a decision
4. an economic system that lets producers answer the three basic questions
5. C.
6. A.
7. C.
8. A.
9. B.

Lesson 2: Introduction to Supply and Demand

1. down
2. down
3. up
4. down
5. up
6. A.
7. B.
8. B.

Lesson 3: Supply and Demand in Action

1. D.
2. C.
3. B.

Lesson 4: Labor and Labor Unions

1. collective bargaining
2. closed shop
3. outsourcing
4. work slowdown
5. labor market
6. B.
7. D.
8. C.

Lesson 5: A Global Economy

1. trading bloc
2. cartel
3. common market
4. trade barrier
5. international trade
6. protectionism
7. free trade
8. globalization

Unit Practice Test

1. What is to be produced?; A construction company decides to specialize in building new strip malls.
2. How is production organized?; An American car company produces its parts in several foreign countries and assembles the finished cars in the United States.
3. For whom are goods and services produced?; A new clothing company decides to market its line of jackets to teenagers and young adults.
4. C.
5. A.
6. B. Because more people want the job with the publishing company, the company can lower the wage.
7. D. Since nobody has the product, the demand is high.
8. A. Since people are not buying the product, demand goes down. Without income from sales, Magnus cannot support his extra ten workers.
9. A.
10.

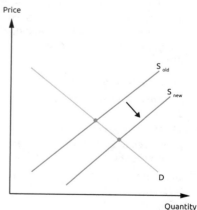

GLOSSARY

abolitionist — person who wanted slaves to be freed

administration — government organized during a president's term

adobe — dried mud brick

Affordable Care Act — law that expanded access to health insurance plans

agenda — plan

alliance — agreement between two or more countries to support each other militarily

allocate — to decide how to use resources

ambassador — person who represents the interests of one country in another country

amendment — changes made to a government document

amnesty — legal forgiveness of people who have committed certain crimes, such as immigrating without proper documentation

ancient Greece — collection of city-states where important political ideas began

ancient Rome — long-ago republic and empire centered on the city of Rome

appeasement — policy of allowing Hitler and the Nazis to take lands that they wanted in Eastern Europe

article — a main section of the U.S. Constitution

Articles of Confederation — first governing document of the United States that gave most power to the states

assembly line — manufacturing process in which workers do the same job all day to help make a finished product together

assimilate — to adapt

average — result found by adding together all of the numbers in a set and dividing the sum by the total number of values in the set

Aztec — people of what is now Mexico who built a city at Tenochtitlan and ruled a large empire

bail — money paid by an accused person to remain free before a trial

bias — personal opinion that shapes how someone views a topic

Bill of Rights — first ten amendments to the U.S. Constitution that protect individual and state rights

bills — proposed laws

birth rate — number of people in a population who are born each year out of 1,000

black codes — laws that unfairly limited rights and opportunities for African Americans

boycott — to refuse to buy

buying power — amount of goods or services that can be bought with a certain amount of money

Cabinet — group of presidential advisers

candidate — person running for political office

caravel — light, mobile Portuguese ship

cartel — organization that controls the supply of a particular good

cash crop — crop grown to sell for a profit

casualties — injuries and deaths in war

checks and balances — way of balancing power among branches so no one becomes too powerful

Citizens United v. Federal Election Commission — 2010 Supreme Court ruling stating that corporations and labor unions could spend unlimited amounts of money on political ads and other tools

Civil Rights Movement — period of people working together to end legalized racial discrimination

citizenship — legal membership of a place

city-state — independent city with its own government and citizenship

civil case — lawsuits that involve disagreements between people

civil liberties — rights that the government is required to protect

civil war — war between groups within a country

climate — usual weather in a place over time

climate change — shifts in climate over time

closed shop — workplace that can hire only union workers; outlawed by the Taft-Hartley Act in 1947

Cold War — competition between the United States and Soviet Union for global power

collective bargaining — process by which employees, represented by their union leaders, negotiate with the employer

Columbian Exchange — movement of plants, animals, and diseases between Europe and the Americas

common currency — currency, such as the Euro, shared among several states

common good — well-being of everyone

GLOSSARY

common market — market in which several countries exchange goods and services without restrictions

communism — system in which resources are owned by everyone and managed by the state

compass rose — map feature showing the map's orientation of north, east, south, and west

concurrent powers — powers shared by the federal and state governments

Congress — national legislature

constitution — plan for government

consumer — person who buys a good or service

consumption — use of goods and services

continent — large landmass

convention — large gathering every four years before the presidential election

cost-push inflation — rise in prices caused by rising costs of labor and other production costs

crime rate — measurement of crimes that happen in a place

cultural diffusion — spread of ideas and practices from place to place

dark money — secret political donations

death rate — number of people in a population who die each year out of 1,000

Declaration of Independence — document announcing American independence from Great Britain

deforestation — widespread cutting down of trees

demand — how much of something consumers want to buy

demand-pull inflation — a rise in prices driven by rising consumer demand

democracy — political system in which citizens vote directly on leaders and laws

demographics — study of populations

derived demand — form of demand that depends on the demand for another good or service

diplomat — person who negotiates with another country

direct democracy — political system in which citizens participate in making all governmental decisions

discrimination — unfair treatment

DREAMer — young, undocumented immigrant who was brought to the United States as a child

due process — proper constitutional procedures in trials and other actions

dynasty — ruling families in which the kingship passes from generation to generation

economic union — combined economic system including many countries, such as the European Union

Electoral College — group of special voters who choose the president

emancipate — to set free

Emancipation Proclamation — executive order that freed all the slaves living in the Confederacy

Enlightenment — period in the 1600s and 1700s that challenged the old ways of thinking about science, religion, and government

enumerated powers — powers of the federal government that are described clearly in the Constitution

Environmental Protection Agency — U.S. government agency that monitors environmental concerns such as air and water pollution

equal protection clause — part of the Fourteenth Amendment requiring states to guarantee the same rights and protections to all citizens

Equal Rights Amendment — proposed constitutional amendment guaranteeing gender equality

Equator — the central line of latitude

exchange — trade

executive branch — branch of U.S. government that enforces laws

export — good sold in a foreign country

extradition — sending a person accused of a crime back to the place in which the supposed crime was committed

federal — U.S. national government

Federal Election Campaign Act — law that limited how campaigns raised money

Federal Election Commission — government agency that monitors all federal election laws and campaign spending

federalism — system of government in which power is spread between national and state or regional units

feminism — women's rights

foreclosure — the taking back of a property by a lender

foreign policy — a country's approach to dealing with other countries

formal region — region with a specific boundary set either by nature or by people

fossil fuel — resources such as coal and oil that are formed from carbon deposits left by decaying life forms from long ago

framers — creators of the U.S. Constitution

156

free trade — system of exchange in which two or more countries conduct trade without barriers such as tariffs

Freedmen's Bureau — federal agency during Reconstruction that set up schools and helped former slaves find new work

free-market system — economic system in which producers and consumers make all economic decisions

French and Indian War — conflict between the British and American colonists on one side and the French and their Native American allies over colonial territory and expansion

Fugitive Slave Act — controversial law that required all U.S. citizens to help capture and return runaway slaves to their owners

full faith and credit — constitutional section stating that each state must cooperate with the other states

functional region — region including all the areas near a place that work together

geography — study of Earth and its people

glacier — large, thick sheet of ice

global positioning system (GPS) — technology that uses satellites to find exact locations

globalization — interconnectedness of people, technology, and ideas around the world

globe — three-dimensional sphere that shows Earth and its features

goods — physical things that can be bought and sold such as books, furniture, and automobiles

Great Compromise — Constitutional compromise dividing Congress into two houses; one house having membership based on a state's population, and the other having two members representing each state

Great Depression — period of worldwide economic downtown during the 1930s

Great Recession — severe economic downturn beginning in the late 2000s and early 2010s

greenhouse gas — gas that traps heat in Earth's atmosphere

guerrilla warfare — style of warfare that uses non-traditional tactics

hard money — money given by individuals or groups directly to candidates

hemisphere — half of Earth

Holocaust — Nazi program in which millions of Jewish people were murdered

human geography — the study of how people interact with broad regional systems

hunter-gatherer — people who survive by collecting wild plants and hunting animals or fish

hurricane — strong storm that forms in the Atlantic Ocean

immigration — movement of people from one place to another in order to live there

impeach — formally accuse of wrongdoing an official from another branch of government

imperialism — use of power by one country to rule another

import — good brought into a country from another

Inca — people who had an empire along the western coast of South America

industrialization — making of goods in factories

inflation — overall increase in prices

infrastructure — systems, like power lines and roads, that connect people

initiative — a ballot measure suggested by the people

interdependence — interrelated nature of economic activities

international organization — global group that promotes a certain goal or idea

international trade — economic exchange conducted between two or more countries

Internet — technology for communicating and sharing information through global computer networks

Iroquois Confederacy — league in which members of some Native American groups agreed to make decisions together and protect one another during wartime

irrigation — systems that move water for farming

Jim Crow laws — laws that unfairly limited voting access and enforced segregation

judicial branch — branch of U.S. government that interprets laws

judicial review — the Supreme Court's ability to find laws or actions unconstitutional

labor — the efforts of workers

labor market — economic system in which workers and employers buy and sell work with wages

GLOSSARY

labor pool — all of the people willing to work or currently working

latitude — imaginary lines encircling Earth horizontally, from east to west

legislative branch — branch of U.S. government that makes laws

legislature — government body that makes laws and decides how the government's money is spent

liberty — freedom

literacy rate — number of people over the age of 15 who can read and write

longitude — imaginary lines that circle Earth vertically, from north to south

Louisiana Purchase — large area of land purchased from France in 1803

Loyalist — Americans who supported the British government and thought the colonial rebellion was a crime

Magna Carta — document that limited the monarch's powers and protected some rights of citizens

manifest destiny — idea that the United States had a duty to expand to the Pacific Ocean

map — tool that displays portions of Earth's features, such as cities or bodies of water, on a flat surface

map projection — the way in which the round Earth is transferred to a flat map

market equilibrium — the point at which supply and demand are equal

Maya — people of northeastern Mexico and Guatemala who built cities centered around huge temples and public buildings

Mayflower Compact — colonial document agreeing that everyone on the *Mayflower* would form together to settle and manage their affairs

McDonaldization — spread of U.S. culture and tastes around the world

mean — average of a set of numbers

median — midpoint of a series of numbers

Mesoamerica — region of Mexico, Central America, and South America settled by people long ago

Middle Colonies — colonies along the Atlantic coastline south of New England

Middle Passage — long, difficult Atlantic crossing that was part of the slave trade

Miranda Warning — official statement by police informing suspects of their rights before questioning

Missouri Compromise — agreement in 1820 that admitted Missouri and Maine as states, and tried to end debate over slavery

mode — value in a set of numbers that occurs most often

multinational corporation — company operating all around the world

municipal — local

natural resource — any useful material provided by Earth

natural rights — rights people are born with, such as life, liberty, and the right to own property

naturalization — process of becoming a citizen of a new place

New Deal — series of federal programs that provided economic help during the Great Depression

New England — American colonies in the far northeast

nomination — selection of candidates for offices

non-renewable resource — resource that cannot be quickly restored and used again

Northwest Ordinance — laws that organized the early American west into territories such as Indiana and Ohio

nuclear bomb — powerful weapon that could flatten entire cities

opportunity cost — what is given up when making an economic choice

ordinance — local law or regulation

outsourcing — sending of jobs to other countries

overturned — reversed

Parliament — British law-making body

perceptual region — region that exists because people think about all the places within it as being similar

physical geography — study of Earth and its landforms, bodies of water, and physical systems

plantation — large farm that grows cash crops

political parties — organized groups that support a set of political beliefs

pollution — any harmful substance that occurs in the environment

popular sovereignty — voting by the people

population — all of the people who live in a place

population pyramid — geographic model showing populations by age bands and gender

Preamble — first part of a document, such as the Declaration of Independence or the U.S. Constitution

precipitation — rain and snowfall

prices — amount charged for goods and services

Prime Meridian — the central line of longitude around the earth

Proclamation of 1763 — British policy setting a western limit for colonial settlement

producer — person who makes and sells goods and services

production — making of goods and services

profits — earnings by producers

Progressives — people who worked for social, political, and economic reform between about 1900 and 1915

protectionism — use of trade barriers to help certain domestic economic goals

quantity demanded — amount of something that consumers are willing to buy at a certain price

quantity supplied — amount of something that producers are willing to sell at a certain price

Quran — holy book of Islam

Radical Republicans — Congressional group during Reconstruction who strongly supported expanding rights for freed slaves in the South

ratify — to formally agree to

raw materials — resources that can be turned into finished products

recall — a vote to remove a politician from office

Reconstruction — period of rebuilding after the Civil War

recycle — to send garbage to be reused as a new item

referendum — a popular vote on a state law or amendment

Reformation — European religious reform movement

region — area with a certain shared characteristic

regulate — to control

Renaissance — period of cultural flowering and rebirth in Europe

renewable resource — resource that can be quickly restored and used again

representative democracy — political system in which citizens vote for leaders who then make laws on their behalf

republic — political system in which citizens vote for leaders who then make laws on their behalf; a representative democracy

republican — form of government in which citizens elect representatives to run the government

reserved powers — powers that stay with the states

resources — materials needed to produce goods and services

runoff election — election held when none of the candidates for an office wins a majority of the vote in the general election

scale — map feature showing distance

scarcity — the condition of not having enough of something for everyone to have what they want and need

school board — group that makes many of the decisions that affect a public school system

Scientific Revolution — time period in the 1500s and 1600s during which scientists challenged old ideas about the world

searches and seizures — investigation or taking of a person's property by the state

secede — formally leave a country

Second Industrial Revolution — period of rapid industrialization and urbanization during the late 1800s

sectionalism — support for the needs of one's own region

segregation — legal separation of people by race

Seneca Falls Convention — 1848 gathering that began the women's rights movement in the United States

separation of powers — idea that governmental powers should be divided among branches to limit one branch from becoming too powerful

services — something a person does for someone else, such as cutting hair or providing medical advice

settlement house — community center that helped immigrants adapt to U.S. society and culture

shortage — too little of something to meet demand

Silk Roads — historical trade routes that connected Asia to the Mediterranean

sit-in — protests in which people entered businesses and refused to leave unless they were served

smallpox —European infectious disease that killed many native people of the Americas

smog — visible air pollution

Glossary

GLOSSARY

soft money — donations that are used for general purposes and do not go to a specific candidate

Southern Colonies — colonies that reached from Virginia southward to the border with Spanish Florida

special district — unit of government that has a key purpose

speculate — to buy something with the intention of selling it later at a profit

states' rights — belief that states, not the federal government, should decide laws about matters within their borders

strike — purposeful work stoppage

suffrage — the right to vote

superpower — country with great political power and influence all around the globe

supply — how much of something producers make

supply shock — sudden shortage of a good or service

supremacy clause — constitutional section stating that the Constitution and federal laws are supreme when in conflict with those of the states

surplus — too much of something to meet demand

Taft-Hartley Act — 1947 law limiting some provisions of the Wagner Act

tariff — special taxes placed on goods brought into a country for sale

telegraph — technology that sent messages quickly over long distances using electricity

terms — periods of time in office

territories — areas controlled by another country

Thomas Jefferson — chief writer of the Declaration of Independence and the third U.S. president

Three-Fifths Compromise — constitutional compromise that allowed three-fifths of the total enslaved population of a state to be counted for purposes of representation in Congress

tolerance — accepting the rights of others to have different opinions and live different lives

tornado — huge column of spinning air

township — land and political subdivision within a county

trade agreement — agreement between two or more countries to conduct trade under certain rules

trade barrier — limit on free trade

trading bloc — group of countries that have free trade with one another

Transcontinental Railroad — long-distance railroad linking the Atlantic and Pacific Oceans

Treaty of Guadalupe-Hidalgo — agreement ending the Mexican-American War that added a great deal of southwestern and western territory to the United States

Treaty of Paris — 1783 agreement that officially gave the United States independence

U.S. Constitution — the highest authority of law in the United States; lists rules as to how the national government operates.

undocumented immigrant — person who comes to the United States without following the proper legal procedures

union — group of workers who join together to increase their power in the labor market

upheld — agreed with

urbanization — growth of cities

utility — usefulness of a particular good or service

verdict — ruling

veto — to reject

violated — to have defied or dishonored

voluntary exchange — buying and selling goods and services

wages — payments for work

Wagner Act — law that guarantees workers the right to organize

weapons of mass destruction — powerful weapons capable of injuring or killing many people at once

weather — measure of the atmospheric conditions, such as temperature, wind, and precipitation, in a place at a certain time

welfare — well-being

women's rights movement — reform movement supporting increased rights and equality for women

work slowdown — purposeful slowing of work by laborers

World Trade Organization — international group dedicated to supporting free trade

Zimmerman Telegram — World War I-era message from Germany to Mexico asking Mexico to declare war on the United States in exchange for helping Mexico reclaim U.S. lands it had once controlled